RIDE IT!

The Complete Book of

TRAIL BIKE RIDING

Printed and bound in England by the publishers

Published by
The Haynes Publishing Group
Sparkford Yeovil Somerset BA22 7JJ England

Soft cover edition **ISBN 0 85696 180 9**
Hard cover edition — *a FOULIS MOTORCYCLING BOOK* — **ISBN 0 85429 221 7**

Editor Jeff Clew
Production/Design Tim Parker
Illustration Terry Davey

RIDE IT!

The Complete Book of

TRAIL BIKE RIDING

Frank
Melling

Foulis

Contents

The author, Frank Melling, with his wife and Fantic enduro machine shows that fun can be had by all when involved with enduro racing and trail riding

Introduction

Gethin Evans is a good friend of mine. Not a mate whom I see every week for a drink at the local; nor one of my racing compatriots from the motocross world, but an exceptionally quick trail rider. Now and again, Gethin and I get together for a day's trail riding and with the Wild Welshman in the lead, we ride hard and fast across the roughest trails available to us, until we have drunk our fill of cross-country motorcycling.

I remember one snow-whipped day in February, Gethin and I rode for virtually six-hours non-stop across the moors and tracks of the Pennines and in all that time, we never saw a single walker, horse rider or even a fellow motorcyclist, and the occasional farmer we came across looked at us as if we were lunatics.

The sleet froze round the edge of our goggles and the bikes slithered around the drowned tracks as we forced them on through the winter gloom. The landscape was bleak and hostile and yet the comforting rhythm of the well-tuned engines, the responsiveness of our purpose-built machines and the sheer pleasure of riding in the company of an expert, combined to give me an inner warmth which defeated all the onslaughts of the winter weather.

At the end of the run, I was physically shattered, too tired to ride another mile and yet, despite the complaints of my body, I was full to contentment with a profound satisfaction which is rare in our modern world. The harshness of the countryside, the unforgiving nature of the terrain and the speed at which we had travelled, had all combined to provide a challenge which, when met and overcome, provided a deeply felt sense of achievement.

Yet to enjoy this sensation, we had not spent more than two or three pounds on petrol and oil, and had neither disturbed nor offended anyone, which made our satisfaction all the more complete, knowing that no-one else had to suffer any inconvenience because of it.

Both Gethin and I are racers first, and trail riders second, and we derive pleasure from trail riding in hard conditions, something which all riders do not, and rightly so.

I was reminded of this one day when I was riding in Wales. Being with a Press colleague, and equipped only with very basic Japanese trail bikes, we were riding a simple track at very modest speeds. In fact, the going was so easy in the dry weather that a Honda 50, sportingly ridden, could have coped easily. Nevertheless, the track went through some very beautiful countryside, with heather-covered hills being cut by many tumbling streams and grey rock shining brightly in the sunshine, having lost all the cold malevolence of winter.

Coming round a bend, we came across a group of trail riders, and after chatting for a while, decided to ride with them. The pace was very easy, and we ambled along in the most leisurely fashion. Every gate which had to be opened was sufficient excuse for a discussion on some subject or other, and I suppose it took us an hour and a half to cover five miles.

When we met the main road again, my friend and I parted company with the group, which went on their way back to the village where they were staying, whilst we headed back towards our van. As they rode away, the same sense of fulfilment that I had felt on that desperate winter trail ride became apparent.

The circumstances were quite different, the tracks provided no challenge, and the weather was idyllic, yet away from the crowds and the tarmac, the trails were offering a balm which many members of our high-pressure, hyper-efficient, technological society spend most of their lives, and a large proportion of their income, trying to acquire.

I have had a lot of pleasure and thrills from motorcycling. I have raced motocross and leaped bikes off jumps and slid them through corners as if my life depended on it — which it sometimes did. On grass-tracks, I have brushed shoulders with opponents at 60mph, and felt my heart hit my boots and then bounce back to my helmet, especially if I was beaten. And having the privilege of the press, I have even had the pleasure of riding in sports outside those which I have made my special interest, and this has led me to Oulton Park aboard hairy road-racing machines, Belle Vue Speedway Stadium, and the wilds of many observed trials sections.

Still, despite all the attractions of these hard core thrill sports, I still have an affection for trail riding. The reason is hard to define, despite much self-analysis, and perhaps this gives a clue to what makes trail riding so attractive to such a wide range of people. Trail riding is whatever you want it to be. Fast and furious — try riding with someone like Gethin Evans and there is no alternative! — or placid and contemplative, absorbing the sense of the countryside as well as the sight, sound and smell. Best of all, it can be fast and furious AND placid in one afternoon, if that is what pleases the rider.

Trail riding is like an open book with blank pages. The rider writes the title and then the trail unfolds the story. Thriller or travel chronicle, bloodthirsty or whimsical - it's up to the author. As I have said, if you decide that the story is not going the way you would like it, then just change the style.

It cannot have been long after the birth of motorcycling that the first rider took his bike trail riding. Of all the forms of man-made transport, only the motorcycle is comfortable and in its element on rough going. Travel along an unmade track in a Land Rover and the ride will consist of being pitched and tossed from side to side as the car wallows along. The caterpillar tracks of a bulldozer will claw the ground apart as it tears its way through any obstacle, but it is the struggle of a patently man-made machine against nature. Then look at a motorcycle over the same terrain. See how it skips from ridge to ridge, how the power lifts the front wheel over obstacles and the rider's body blends into the machine, to make an almost individual entity. The bike is still only so much rubber, steel and alloy, but somehow, it manages to transcend the restraints imposed on every other vehicle, and take on the personality of a living creature. The Spanish Bultaco factory described this phenomenon as the 'mechanical horse' — a concept which captures the spirit of the motorcycle beautifully and also explains why trail riding, under various guises, has always been an integral part of motorcycling.

Riding a 'mechanical horse' is fun. Thousands of new motorcyclists discover this fact every year. The ease of handling and responsiveness of a motorcycle on the road is unequalled, and it must be one of the few vehicles on our modern roads which is still actually a pleasure to drive. What was once something of a secret, but is now becoming more widely known, is that riding a bike on the rough is more fun than riding one on the road.

At one time, a machine that would explore the tracks and green lanes of Britain would have had to be heavy and difficult for a non-expert rider to handle. It would have had required much maintenance and would have been hard to start and often unreliable. Now, modern lightweight machines are freely and cheaply available, which take the rider on any expedition he wishes to undertake, without making vast demands on his riding skill. As late as 1965, the trails were the province of an elite band of enthusiasts — now they are freely available to everyone.

What use the thousands of miles and tracks that are legally available are put to, rests with the rider. Some will want to pit their riding skills against terrain where only a motorcycle, or a fit man on foot, could traverse. Others will want to explore the quiet and secluded lanes, where an escape from the pressures of modern life may be found. There is room for both points of view and every other shade of opinion for, in Britain, we are fortunate in having ample opportunity for everyone to drink his fill of whatever trail riding brew satisfies his thirst.

The other aspect of trail riding which I find satisfying is that it seems to attract a very pleasant section of the community. Whether by accident or intent, trail riders are invariably some of the most tolerant and easy going characters in the motorcycling world.

Many of them have helped with the preparation of this book and this advice and constructive criticism has been much appreciated. Now, not only do I owe a debt of thanks to all those riders who have rescued me from bottomless bogs, but also an equal number whose experience and knowledge has contributed so much to this book.

1 Off road riding

Strictly speaking, trail riding is a pastime which involves riding a motorcycle along unsurfaced roads. However, whilst this might be the letter of the law, it is not an adequate description of one of motorcycling's most pleasurable facets, for as we have already seen, trail riding embraces a wide range of riding styles and terrain. A two foot wide sheep track wending its way up the side of a precipitous Welsh crag is as much a trail as one of the motorway-wide routes across the Wiltshire Downs and both, in their own way, are just as enjoyable.

Similarly, trail riders, or green laners, are as diverse a section of the community as you are likely to meet. Some are strongly opposed to any form of trail riding which has the slightest hint of a competitive element, maintaining that it is a pastime and to tarnish it with racing devalues the inherent attraction of quiet, thoughtful riding. Furthermore, they acknowledge that it incurs the wrath of such organisations as The Rambler's Association which, given the opportunity, would like to convince the authorities that all trail riders are tearing across the countryside and should be banned from the trails where we can now ride legally.

Other riders use trail riding as practice for competition and rarely, if ever, are satisfied unless they are pitting their machines against the toughest terrain at the highest possible speeds. Personally, I fall somewhere in between, finding pleasure both in the gentle ride through soft countryside and also from struggling against tough conditions.

To a newcomer, the perplexing assortment of nomenclatures which describe different facets of trail riding and tracks must cause bewilderment. A lot of the difficulty arises from the fact that trail riding has only enjoyed mass popularity since the advent of light, reliable and relatively cheap motorcycles on which to ride — probably since around the early 1970s. Hard men can, and did, traverse the tracks on their AJS and Ariel machines, but hauling 300 lb of motorcycle about was not most people's idea of fun, particularly when an Honours degree in engineering was a useful asset in order to keep the bike running.

With the boom in trail riding, and the addition of many terms from the American motorcyclist's vocabulary, trail riding has developed its very own jargon which, deriving from the vernacular, is not always consistent in meaning. A further conundrum which adds to the fun is that trail riding, as we have shown, is a wide-embracing activity which means many things to many riders — and on numerous occasions even the speaker offering the definition will not be sure precisely what he means.

Let us begin by placing trail riding in context with the other forms of motorcycle sport which are carried on off-road. In calling trail riding a sport, rather than a pastime, I hope that I have not offended anyone, but if as peaceful and physically inactive an activity as angling deserves to be called Britain's leading participant sport, then I am sure that something as much non-stop fun as trail riding qualifies equally well.

Motorcycling's premier sport, and certainly the king of all the off-road activities, is motocross — and I write that statement as an unbiased observer who, coincidentally, has spent the last twelve years racing. In motocross, the rider has to compete against his opponents on a track which will involve downhill jumps, cambers, 60mph straights and bone-jarring leaps. Having tried most forms of motorcycle sport, I can honestly say that it is the most demanding, both physically and mentally — and also the most satisfying. Motocross is also expensive, and demands a degree of physical fitness which most professional athletes will not achieve.

Occasionally, trail riders will be accused of scrambling (the old term for motocross) and vigilance must be high if they are to avoid this. Motocross is fast and furious, and is only safe on a specially enclosed track, which the riders have studied very carefully before competing on, and from which the public are kept at a safe distance.

1:50,000 series Ordnance Survey maps are some of the most vital pieces of equipment a rider has at his disposal

Obviously, to treat a public track like a motocross course would be foolish in the extreme, as well as dangerous to the rider. I have yet to see any trail rider behaving like this and I ride with some hard men. Should you come across this sort of uninformed comment then it is as well for all of us that you can refute it easily and knowledgeably.

Grass-tracking is a distant cousin of motocross and a closer relative of speedway. The tracks are usually oval and on more or less smooth grassland. The technique is to slide the big, alcohol-burning bikes around the corners, which are always left-handed, in speedway style, and racing is very spectacular for both competitors and spectators. Trail bikes will slide, but they are difficult to ride in the full-throttle, opposite-lock power slides which grassers manage. If you do become proficient at sliding your 125cc Kawasaki, then it might be better to forget trail riding, and buy a big, hairy 500cc grass track machine and try to become a second Peter Collins.

Many of the virtues of the observed trials rider are to be found in a skilful trail rider, for in this sport the objective is to traverse very difficult terrain at slow speeds, without either stopping the motorcycle, or aiding progress by using the feet for balance. A top-class trials rider is a joy to behold, for he will be capable of piloting his bike over terrain upon which most humans could not even walk. Better still, he will make the exercise look as easy as riding on smooth tarmac.

Throttle control, an ability to judge terrain for grip and firmness and total concentration, are the traits which makes a successful trials rider. Obviously, a trials rider on his light, easy to handle bike, will find no difficulty with even the most severe trails, and many riders who began off-road riding on the green lanes, take a liking to this challenging form of motorcycling sport. Occasionally, there are classes for trail bikes in an observed trial, and this is a good opportunity to find out just how well you can handle your bike with a sensitive throttle hand.

Britain provides some of the most interesting off-road riding in the world. These two riders are about to start an excursion along one of the many thousands of miles of RUPPs

However, the sport to which most trail riders aspire, is enduros. The term is an American one for a long distance reliability trial in which the rider has to travel many miles — as many as 150 in a day — over rough tracks, open moorland, rocky climbs and rivers, at a set average speed. As soon as he falls below that speed, he accrues marks which count against him. At the end of the day, the rider with the lowest total marks wins, and there are awards for a percentage of the riders coming closest to this score.

Many experienced competitors think that enduros, above all other forms of motorcycle sport, are the supreme test of all-round riding ability. In an enduro, the rider will have to be part motocrosser and part trials rider. If he is to be a medal winner, he will also have to be more than a little of a road-racer on the Forestry sections closed to the public, where there are no speed limits and all traffic, except competitors, is banned.

Enduros are very tough on both riders and machines but their great attraction is that they can be sensibly entered on a well-prepared trail bike. All the other sports mentioned, with the exception of special classes in observed trials, need expensive machinery which is peculiar to that branch of motorcycling. Motocross in particular, demands light and extremely powerful bikes with sophisticated suspension, all of which make for a costly purchase. Grass bikes are equally specialised, although not nearly as expensive, but like motocrossers, they cannot be used for anything except their particular form of racing. However, a trail bike can be used for pleasure every weekend and for competition when the opportunity arises. Care is needed to prepare the bike properly but this is possible, as we will discuss in Chapter 11.

The four off-road sports we have briefly examined all make particular (and usually expensive) demands on the rider, and often limit him as to what he can do with his bike when he has mortgaged his house and sold the dog to get it. Even a trials bike, which is legal for use on the road, is somewhat limited, for no-one but an arch-enthusiast would willingly ride a trials bike on tarmac, since they are designed to be ridden primarily with the rider in the standing position and any comfort offered is of the most spartan nature.

Trail riding, whilst not having the glamour of racing, is clearly the best value when one divides the hours of riding into the cost of the bike and subsequent running costs. Also the price of even a sophisticated trail bike is hundreds of pounds less than that of a motocross machine and also considerably cheaper than either a grass bike or an observed trials iron. Better still, it is quite possible to have a lot of fun on a hundred pound bike, riding the green lanes, whilst this sum would hardly purchase a cylinder barrel and piston for a MX'er. You will never have a fan club, even if you turn out to be the world's best trail rider, but by the same token, you can ride 52 weeks a year and still remain solvent.

We in Britain are blessed with having the best off-road riding in the world. I once rode with an American friend from Idaho, who had ridden up and down vast sand dunes, through remote forests and over precipitous trails and yet he was more pleased with an afternoon's riding in Derbyshire than with any of these exotic ventures. The reason, he explained, was the variety of British tracks, for we saw more interesting features and experienced a wider range of terrain in fifteen miles than he could see in a month's riding in America. Not that I don't long to blast over a seventy foot sand dune or spend a week exploring some wild mountain range, but this would be a tremendous addition to what we already have in Britain, certainly not a substitute.

At present, we can ride legally over thousands of miles of tracks and trails in Britain. This is as much a right as any other law on the statute books, and it is the envy of motorcyclists all over the world. The RIGHT IN LAW to ride is of inestimable value and it must be jealously guarded, for sadly, there are certain misguided elements of the community who would take this right from us in the name of preserving the countryside. For this reason, it is vital that every rider knows where he can, and cannot, ride within the law, and behaves in a responsible fashion when he is trail riding. I have yet to see a trail rider cause any trouble to any member of the public or inflict any damage to the track — and I can say this with hand on heart. Even so, we are under constant pressure, and this when no offence has been committed. How much more vitriolic would be the attacks if riders were to behave irresponsibly?

For this reason, the rest of the chapter is an attempt to clarify where a rider can use his bike legally and although it may not make the most palatable of reading, it is as vital as any of the other chapters on buying a bike or machine preparation — vital both to the individual rider and to the whole sport. If this sounds rather melodramatic, then believe me it is not. Every rider has a vital responsibility to the whole sport and even one slip can cause repercussions out of all proportion to the "crime".

Let us begin by sorting out the various synonyms which are used to describe the areas where a motorcycle can be ridden off-road. Most of these areas are called "trails" — hence "trail riding" — but the more traditional name, and the one which is still in common use, is "green lanes". Both of these terms refer to the Roads Used As Public Pathways, which is the legal definition of a strip of land, that is, an unsurfaced road along which

Some of the lesser used RUPPs can provide a real challenge to riding skills — and provide the most fun

vehicular traffic may pass. Just to confuse the matter even more, many good trails are called tracks within the trail riding fraternity, and sometimes a track may be on private land and its use restricted to those riders who have the owner's permission. I have permission to ride on a number of such tracks and these are completely outside the jurisdiction of the law. If I wished, after obtaining the land-owner's agreement, I could ride my unsilenced, unregistered motocross machine along them, since I am riding on private property which has no access for the public. I do not ride a motocross machine along them because the noise would soon lose me the privilege of riding there and also walkers might see the bike and mistake it for a trail bike. Racing machines with nominal silencers are suitable only for use on closed circuits where the public expects, and welcomes, the noise as an integral part of the activity.

Sorting through the mass of esoteric vocabulary, often carrying dual meanings, is difficult for anyone and must be a challenging proposition for the newcomer to the sport. Perhaps the best way to approach the problem is to do a trail riding dance of the Seven Veils, stripping away the bits we do not want, that is identifying where we cannot ride and then getting down to the job, of riding of course.

First and foremost, you may not ride your bike over private property, without permission. This is trespass, and in addition to the penalties laid down by the law, an erring rider may find himself forcibly ejected by the owner. As well as getting himself into trouble, one foolish act can often cause endless trouble for a lot of motorcyclists who were completely innocent, and may undo a lot of good public relations work done by riders over many years.

Secondly, you may not ride on footpaths. The right of way on these paths is for pedestrians only and is jealously guarded by them. Very often, footpaths are not suitable for bikes, but sometimes they can be very tempting. Take notice of the green and white signs, which will state quite clearly that they are to be used by walkers only.

Finally, there are the bridle paths, which are something of a sore point with many motorcyclists. These tracks are for use by horse riders (and pedestrians of course), but exclude motorcycles. One is tempted to think that when the tracks were designated, there was more than a little bias against motorcyclists, since many of the bridle paths are eminently suitable for bikes and could be quite easily enjoyed by followers of both pastimes. However, despite their attractiveness, bridle paths are out of bounds, and there are penalties in law for using them.

By this time there are no doubt feelings of despondency creeping into the hopeful trail rider's mind but although there are bounds on exactly where a motorcycle may be ridden, they are not so stringent as to be prohibitive or discouraging. The key to trail riding in Britain is a knowledge of the RUPPs. These, as has been mentioned already, are Roads Used As Public Pathways and are sprinkled around the country. They are shown on the Ordnance Survey Maps as a red, broken line, with alternating semi-circles. They are taken from the definitive maps for an area and show a public right of way for all vehicles. That is, you may ride up and down one of these roads until your bike wears out and no-one can, or will, bother you.

Some RUPPs can run for miles and others for only a few hundred yards, before joining on to another track, or petering out. If another track is shown on the ordnance survey map, and is not marked as a RUPP, then there is no guaranteed right of way and there may, or may not be, passage for a motorcycle.

In referring to Ordnance Survey Maps, I am talking about what amounts to the trail rider's "holy book", for these superb maps are the key to trail riding. Without them, the sport would be much more laborious and certainly not as open to non-experts as it is at present.

The scale of the maps is 1:50,000 and they will quite literally show individual houses or even outbuildings on a farm. In addition to finding RUPPs, a rider can also tell, by looking at the contour lines shown, whether the trail is likely to be a good one, before he even gets to see it. Closely bunched contours mean a steep climb and a challenging ride for the experienced rider, or perhaps a warning sign to the newcomer. They also show rivers, streams, fords and known marsh lands and again, this can be invaluable information to anyone planning a trail ride

In addition to the RUPPs shown on the Ordnance Survey maps, there will be other roads with a public right of way. These will only be shown on the definitive maps of the county, usually kept in the County Surveyor's Office. Access should be available to these by members of the public, and a diligent rider could establish whether he is legally permitted to ride on a section of a track.

This right of way spotting is almost a sport in itself, and some riders make a full time hobby of discovering whether a particular track has right of way or not. It is not a facet of trail riding which appeals to me personally, but I am very grateful to all those enthusiasts who are diligent map students and can consequently put up a stiff fight when any of our riding rights is threatened.

If a rider is prepared to sacrifice some of his pride, interesting terrain can be found almost anywhere. This picture was taken only four miles from the centre of a major industrial town

Britain is one of the few countries which actually provides facilities for trail riding. Note that only motorcycles are permitted on this track

In practice, any rider who strays from an RUPP marked on an Ordnance Survey map, on to a track which has no right of way but carries no warning notices to this effect, is unlikely to be prosecuted or even meet with any hostility. Should a farmer stop you and point out that you have erred, then try to accept his comments with good grace and invariably, all will be well. Often a five minute chat will reveal fresh riding ground, if it is conducted in a reasonable manner, and the trouble invariably occurs only when the motorcyclist, sometimes under pressure from a belligerent assailant, starts giving as good as he gets. Soon tempers rise and motorcyclists en masse, are branded as trouble makers.

One of the best ways of discovering good trail riding ground is to follow an observed trial. Often the sections on these trials are linked by RUPPs and it is possible to have a pleasant day's trail riding, following the route of the trial and watching the skills of the feet up experts. One word of warning (it seems that there is always some proviso with every opportunity to ride a trail); an observed trial may make use of private land, hard won ground which is loaned, or hired, specially for the event. No-one will mind a sensibly ridden trail bike using the ground, whilst the event is in progress, but do remember that the land ceases to be fair game at the end of the day. Not only will the trespass incur the wrath of the farmer, and the long arm of the law, but I know a number of club secretaries who will take great delight in personally nailing an erring rider to the nearest tree for jeopardizing their trials land by indiscriminate use.

This is not to say that all private land is out of bounds — quite often the contrary is the case. I know of two hill farmers in the Derbyshire area who, for a nominal sum, will allow trail riders free access to almost all their land. In the case of one chap, there is almost enough land to run an enduro. He is in fact, host to two scrambles courses, run by different clubs, and regular observed trials. Last time I rode on his farm he charged £1 for three of us, which was a bargain on any terms. You may not be so lucky in your area but with tact, discretion and patience, plus a quiet bike, it is surprising how open-minded many farmers can be.

So far, the trails we have been discussing are those which would please a purist. Depending on its location, a RUPP could contain steep climbs, forestry tracks, rocks, fords and a real deep country atmosphere. This is the way to go trail riding in style and is obviously the ideal to seek. Unfortunately, if one is based in an urban conurbation, then regular riding on "proper" trails may be out of the question because of the time and cost involved in reaching them. However, all is not lost, for a rider with an open mind as to what constitutes a trail, and a keen eye for an unlikely riding area, can often find a tasty snack to satisfy his appetite for riding.

An example of one such spot was some waste ground belonging to the Manchester Ship Canal Company at Irlam, right in the midst of the Greater Manchester conurbation. This land was composed of dredgings from the Ship Canal that had been dumped to form about 10 acres of humps and mounds on which I spent many happy hours when I first started rough riding.

At the time, our activities had the blessing of the Ship Canal Company and the arrangement seemed ideal. Unfortunately, too many scramblers with unsilenced machines — the land was surrounded by high density housing — caused too much trouble and the CWS margarine factory complained that its office girls were being distracted by the big he-men riders leaping their bikes about and the riding had to stop. However, if good land can be found in Irlam, then I am confident it can be found anywhere.

Some purists will scorn the thought of taking their beloved trail bikes on to canal dredgings, with a steel works belching smoke and sulphur fumes as a backdrop, and I would agree that it certainly lacks something compared with mid-Wales in June. However, faced with the prospect of being proud and not riding, and taking the opportunity to ride on the rough, you will always find me with my leg across a bike, even if the track is only the access road to an isolated maggot farm. Incidentally, I do know of such a track which happens to be a very good couple of miles' riding, if the rider does not have a sensitive nose.

2 What is a trail bike?

A good trail bike is one which carries its rider over the terrain he wishes to ride, in a manner which pleases him. This simple axiom is the quintessence of all the manifold criteria by which trail bikes are judged.

If the most gentle of green lanes are going to be the main cross-country going, together with a good proportion of road work, then the bike will not need to be far removed from a roadster. However, if the rider wishes to pit himself against the ruthless courses which are plotted by enduro organisers, he will need a highly specialised mount designed expressly to deal with these conditions.

In practice, most trail riders will find a bike erring towards the roadster end of the spectrum far more suitable than a motocross machine with lights. Most competition machines are expensive to buy, require a lot of maintenance, and can be a handful for the newcomer to trail riding. Their purchase, whilst often superficially attractive, should be given much thought.

Having stated that a successful trail bike is one which satisfies its rider, a discussion of the criteria by which most riders judge their machines would seem to be fruitful. Initially, I have selected four separate headings, which will give us a basic yardstick by which we can measure a cross-country bike, and also provide an insight into the tasks the machine will be expected to perform.

General criteria for judging trail bikes

1   The engine should be reliable under all conditions. It should start easily at all times, even if frequently stopped, and particularly if stalled.
2   The engine should have a good spread of power and be pleasant to use in adverse conditions.
3   The motorcycle should have good ground clearance.
4   The motorcycle should be quiet.

Let me commence by saying that of all the points, number four is the most important. Whatever else a trail bike can, or cannot do, unless it performs quietly, it is a menace to everyone. Britain is a tiny island and it is grossly unfair to expect everyone to be annoyed for the sake of a small number of riders' pleasure. More important is that public opinion will not tolerate noisy bikes in the countryside, no matter how well they are ridden or what courtesies their riders show. If trail riding is to be freely permitted, then it is the first duty of every rider to guarantee that his machine gives no offence. Failure to do this will put the hangman's noose around the neck of the sport, without any shadow of doubt.

It is well worth adding that a sensible rider can, by judicious use of the throttle when riding in sensitive areas, reduce whatever level of noise his machine produces. Revving the bike flat out through the gears will make even the most well muffled machine produce an unacceptable level of noise and really this style of riding is quite unnecessary for normal trail riding or even racing in enduros. Changing gear just 2,000rpm below peak revs will bring down the noise to a level which the great majority of the public will find quite acceptable and this in turn means that our right to make ANY noise with trail bikes will be protected.

Turning from this vital, but rather sombre subject, let us look at what makes a fun trail bike. I put reliability at the top of the list. If the bike keeps going, regardless of conditions, then it is possible to forgive it an awful lot. I rode a 'works' ISDT Husqvarna — a six-speed 125cc model — which was really hard work. The narrow power band meant that keeping going in tricky conditions was a full time job, but the way that the

At one end of the trail riding spectrum is this beautiful 125cc ISDT Husqvarna. It has six speeds, is capable of 80 mph and uses petrol at a frightening rate. It also has to be kept revving above 6000 rpm to produce any useable power. This could be the bike for you but it could also pose many problems

engine just kept buzzing away, no matter how brutally it was treated, brought tears of admiration to my eyes. Whatever other faults it had, it could be relied upon to keep going no matter what, and this compensated for many of its weaknesses.

A trail bike can be reasonably expected to get liberally splashed in water, if not immersed in it. The water will come from streams or fords which are commonplace on the better trails; from extensive puddles and flooded areas of the track, and through very heavy rain which is prevalent in mountains and hills, particularly in winter, when much trail riding takes place. The ignition and air filtration system must be adequate to prevent the ingress of water.

One of the great pleasures of trail riding is stopping. Halts are frequent, to look at things of interest; for consultation of maps; to open and close gates or merely to enjoy the pleasure of being out in the wilds. Whatever the reason, the bike's engine should not be fussy about re-starting easily on the kickstart. A trail bike which requires a spark plug to be changed, or a long push before it can be persuaded into life, is fun for neither the owner nor his companions.

Unless you are a brilliant rider, who never midjudges a section of ground, or takes the wrong path through a bog, it is important that your bike starts well if you stall it. Some competition machines, in particular, suffer from a disease known as 'gassing up' which means that they will be reluctant to start until fresh mixture has been forced through the engine by the rider's efforts at the kickstart. This can be a frustrating job if you are trying desperately not to disappear into the stomach of a 70 foot-deep primaeval bog at the same time as kicking the bike.

The Husqvarna I quoted earlier could also serve as an example of the power characteristics a trail bike should NOT have. The Husky would cough and splutter at much below 6,000rpm and it required a true racing best from it. A good trail bike should have plenty of pulling power from low rpm, and the power delivery should be progressive, without any noticeable surge.

The Husky has superb handling, providing it is driven hard

Flat out jumps are no problem either, but is this how you want to trail ride?

The ideal is often difficult to achieve with the smaller machine, since their engines are highly tuned to give very high power outputs from a small capacity. Most 125cc machines will perform much better at high revs, than lower in the rev range, simply because their engines need to turn over quickly in order to produce the power. In this case, a motor must be sought which has sufficient mid-range and bottom end power to free the rider from the worry of having the motor cut out (in trail riding parlance, the term used is die), and also provide sufficient pulling power to make slow speed riding in low gears pleasant.

What we are looking for in practice, is an engine which is easy to use in adverse conditions. Any trail bike will be happy on a smooth dirt road in the middle of July. The good engine is the one which will drag you out of a muddy rut in the height of a December blizzard, without any fuss or bother.

An engine which fits this description perfectly is the Honda 50 — the unit which powers the 'U' frame runabouts. This engine is absolutely reliable, never tires, and keeps going under extremely adverse conditions. Unfortunately, it lies only six inches from the ground and is prone to drowning at the first hint of a real trail puddle. A number of my friends used to play about on pseudo-trail Honda 50s because they could be bought very cheaply and required no maintenance, but none of them were ever successful because they lacked ground clearance. A 4 inch deep rut would put the Honda's engine firmly on the ground and progress would grind to a halt — and 4 inch ruts are in the baby class on some stretches of road that I know.

About 9 clear inches beneath the crankcase is about right, since this will give enough ground clearance to negotiate most obstacles, yet will keep the weight sufficiently low to give good handling.

Although 9 inches ground clearance is adequate for trail riding, the author's Suzuki is near to the ideal with 11 inches

Collecting the impressions from the discussion of these criteria, we form a picture of a quiet, tractable machine with a reliable engine, well shielded from the elements, and having a fairly good ground clearance. Except for the ground clearance, there would be very little to indicate that we were looking at a trail bike. Yet, a trail bike is a special machine, and to be a successful tool for serious cross-country riding, it does require a marked degree of specialization. However, what form this specialization takes is wide, wide open and one of the nicest things about trail bikes is the range of sizes and shapes that successful machines come in.

Most bikes do have certain features in common, and it would be advantageous to discuss these and then see how they are applied in actual production machines.

Perhaps the most important items which every trail bike should have are purpose designed wheels and tyres. Most road-bikes have 18 inch or 19 inch diameter wheels, and are fitted with tyres of approximately the same section. This sytem is perfect for travelling on the road, but would be woefully inadequate on the rough because the front and rear wheels of the trail bike have quite different functions and need to be of different sizes, if they are to work satisfactorily.

An 18 inch wheel fitted to the front of a motorcycle negotiating ruts and bumps will punish the rider severely, by smelling out every single hole and plummeting into it. This reduces rider control to a great degree, and makes the ride most uncomfortable. Further, to maintain a high degree of manoeuvrability, a narrow section tyre is needed. This will normally be of 2.75 inch or 3.00 inch, but some of the smaller bikes (wrongly in my opinion) carry a 2.25 inch tyre. In all cases, the rim size must be 21 inch diameter.

The rear wheel of the bike will have to provide drive in all conditions, including wet clay, slimy mud or moss covered stone. To maximise the machine's power, a large section rear tyre — usually 4.00 inch, 4.60, or even 5.00 inch — is fitted, but this time using an 18 inch rim. If this seems hypocritical after the explanation of the benefits of having an 18 inch rear rim, let me go on to say that only the mechanical restraints of getting a large rim, and wide tyre, together with a lot of suspension movement, all crammed into the tight confines of the bike's rear sub-frame, prevent designers from adopting a large rim. Much more drive would be available with a 21 inch rear rim since the tyre would turn more slowly on any given gearing, thus increasing traction, than would be the case with an 18 inch unit. Also, the same arguments which made the 21 inch front wheel so much better over bumps, would hold true for the rear wheel. In fact, 22 inch rear wheels, but with narrow section tyres, are used on a lot of 1,000 metre grass track machines, in order to increase drive on the loose tracks used for this form of racing.

To go with the wheels, either trails tyres or full 'knobblies' must be used, if anything other than the mildest of trails is to be attempted. A trails tyre has a square profile and a bold block pattern quite unlike any road tyre. This type of tyre can be made to give quite exceptional traction on very bad surfaces, if the rider has

The difference between knobbly (motocross pattern) and trials tyres is well illustrated in this photograph. Knobblies are essential for racing but not for trail riding. Genuine enduro tyres are better than ordinary motocross tyres although the best combination for ultra-serious racing is a 500" x 18" Dunlop MotoCross rear and 3.00" x 21" Metzeler Enduro front. This set-up is also the most expensive — some £30 in 1976

good throttle control. These tyres are obligatory for all competitors in observed trials, and exponents of this sport can perform amazing feats, whilst using them. They are also satisfactory for trail riding, providing some discretion is used. Because trials tyres have a square profile, they do not give good traction at high angles of lean — particularly when travelling quickly — and so cornering hard on the rough can cause problems. Similarly, hard braking is not possible with a trials tyre, since the blocks of the tread pattern do not bite into the ground in the way that a full knobbly does.

However, for most trail riding, conducted at touring speeds, the trials tyre is perfectly adequate and even has a number of advantages. Because its tread form is not as fierce as the knobbly, it does not cause nearly so much damage to green lanes: this in itself is an excellent reason for using trials tyres. Wear will also be far better than a knobbly, which can be ruined in a thousand miles of mixed going, and it is also cheaper to purchase initially. Finally, the trials tyre is far better behaved on tarmac than is a knobbly, which has a habit of breaking traction very fiercely when used on metalled roads.

Knobbly tyres are designed for motocross racing, and they perform best on the trails when used in the manner which most nearly approximates their designer's original intention. To ride quickly on green lanes, it is essential to be able to stop, corner, and accelerate hard and at will. This is what the motocross tyre offers the skilled rider. It offers the less skilled a chance to obtain good traction, even with relatively clumsy throttle control and it will provide a useful lifebelt in really bad conditions, which would otherwise incapacitate the machine.

A suspension system that is either competition orientated, or derived from experience in this field, is a great help. Again, the criterion which will fail or pass a suspension is speed. Ridden with dignity, a machine with quite basic suspension will be quite happy on the trails. However, the faster the rider wishes to travel, the more he will depend on first class suspension, both at the front and the rear of the bike.

The best suspension systems are those derived from motocross machines and the front forks of such machines will have at least 7 inches of well damped travel. At the rear, the most modern machines with angled rear dampers will have a similar sort of travel, whilst bikes with conventionally placed dampers will offer around 4½ inches of movement.

21 inch front and 18 inch rear wheels fitted with knobbly tyres. Note that the front tyre is much narrower than the rear. Also the hubs on both wheels are small and light, although still very powerful

Only the very best competition type trail bikes will have such good suspension and any machine which offers 5 inches of smooth, progressive front fork action should be considered perfectly adequate. It is crucial to remember that not only is the amount of movement important but the action should be of a kind which is usable. If it is too soft, or equally too hard, then all the available movement will not be used.

Since speeds will be low, even in competition, there is no need for the immense brakes which are often found on road machines. Small hubs of 5 inch or 6 inch housing single leading shoe brakes, are ideal, providing ample retardation together with the good sensitivity which is so essential for braking on slippery surfaces. Brakes designed from racing experience, which are water resistant, are a great help, as are the waterproof linings, which can be fitted to most bikes.

The air-filtration must be soundly designed — particularly with regard to waterproofing. The intake should be placed as high as possible on the frame and should be well protected from water thrown up from the rear tyre. It is difficult to imagine just how much water can be directed at an air-filter intake during the course of a quite ordinary trail ride, but it is certainly far more than even the most severe bad weather road journey is likely to inflict.

The access covers to the air-filter element should also be protected, to prevent the ingress of water, as should the connection between the filter box and carburettor. In other words, every conceivable, and very often every inconceivable, way that water can work its way into the induction system must be protected. A good manufacturer will do this in his original design, and leave only the finishing touches to the rider. A lesser bike will place the onus almost entirely on the owner. Protecting the filtration system from water will automatically mean that it is also proof against mud and other species of larger debris. A foam filter element will ensure that fine dust does not find its way into the engine.

If a bike has all the features we have discussed so far, then it will qualify as a very sound trail bike. After this, we can start looking for luxury features which, whilst not essential, are nice to have on a cross-country machine.

Crankcase shields are of less value than most people believe, unless the bike is being used in really severe conditions. Most trails do not require the obligatory traversing of extremely large boulders — so large that a bike equipped with the wheels we have discussed and a 9 inch ground clearance, is going to foul them, if ridden slowly. Tackle the same rocks at speed, and the ensuing shock will depress the suspension and then a crankcase guard will really be needed, but in most cases, it serves only as insurance. Nevertheless, it is nice to have some sort of protection for the engine's vital parts, and this is a good way of providing it.

Crankcase shields are useful. This KTM has a neat and light unit which is very effective. Note also the lip at the front of the shields which deflects much of the mud and water which would otherwise hit the cylinder barrel

Similar protection can be provided for the rider, by the fitting of a ¾ competition saddle designed for fast riding across rough country. Regardless of how slowly you wish to traverse the green lanes, it still pays dividends to look to the motocross world for your saddle, since designers in this field have long since produced many excellent seats — long, firm and comfortable — which will save you from the exquisite agonies of buttocks pummelled into submission by a long day's trail riding.

When the time comes to fall off, as it inevitably will, it is nice to have footrests which fold on impact, rather than centre-punch the rider's leg, as a rigidly mounted unit will try to achieve. The footrests should fold up and back at a 45º angle, and be spring loaded so that they return quickly to their normal position, when released. Such footrests are also very useful for squeezing the bike through very narrow gaps, which rigid footrests would foul, and of course, they will bend up of their own volition if the bike is dropped heavily, rather than ripping the frame apart.

Lights, which every trail bike should have in full working order, should be tucked away so that they have as much protection as possible in a fall. A stone guard covering the front light is a good idea, as is a rubber mounting of the rear light — an item which suffers much from the stresses of vibration.

Last, but not least, should be some form of protection for the chain. Incredible as it may seem to most trail riders, a chain running in an oil bath will transmit very large bhp outputs without the slightest need for any adjustment, in hundreds of hours of non-stop movement. Compare this with the sagging chains that proliferate the paddock after a 150 mile enduro. The sole reason for this horrific rate of chain wear is the unhealthy conditions in which the chains of trail bikes are expected to function.

A chain is effectively a long string of roller bearings and the worst possible conditions in which a bearing can operate are water and mud: just the conditions that the rear chain of a trail bike normally finds itself. Not surprisingly, chain wear is extremely high and that is both inconvenient and also very expensive.

A complete solution is easily achieved, but all too seldom applied. If the chain is totally enclosed, then it is protected from the elements, and if occasional lubrication is applied, it will last virtually indefinitely. For some strange reason best known to themselves, few manufacturers apply this method of protection — Jawa, MZ and Bultaco being the notable exceptions — and seek alternative, and far less satisfactory, solutions.

Folding footrests are vital to avoid injury to the rider and damage to the bike

A typical Japanese rear light assembly as it leaves the factory. Heavy and solidly mounted, it is not designed for trail use

A much better unit is this little Aprilla rear light which is flexibly mounted on a strip of canvas backed rubber so that it will absorb a lot of punishment without damage

Chains suffer tremendous wear when used on the rough. Ideally, they should be fully enclosed, as shown on this ISDT Jawa. These machines can do 1500 racing miles under the most arduous conditions, with virtually no attention

The best of these alternatives is the fitting of an extensive chainguard, which protects the chain from the spray thrown up by the tyres.'Tyre-wash', as this phenomenon is known, will effectively and ruthlessly strip the chain of its vital lubricant — whether in grease or oil form — in a few miles, leaving the rollers to wear very quickly.

Some of the better bikes have a small oil tank which feeds a metered quantity of oil continuously on to the chain. This sytem has the dual advantages of providing fresh and uncontaminated lubricant and also removing a certain quantity of debris from the chain. Its disadvantage is that the oil is not guaranteed to penetrate to the rollers and in practice, often does not.

Worst of all, and to be avoided at all costs, is a chain protected by the legal minimum of cover along its top run. Not only will such a guard not keep water off the chain but it will also permit free access to abrasive mud — a combination which can annihilate the best chain in the world with amazing ease.

Although by now it might seem that no manufacturer could ever build a bike which can meet our criteria, this is far from the case. Jawa build a trail bike which not only meets, but exceeds, all the standards we have discussed in this chapter. The only difficulty is that an ISDT Jawa is virtually unobtainable by a private owner, and is so fast that most riders would scare themselves silly trying to ride one. At the other end of the spectrum there are, it must be admitted, a number of machines whose only concession to trail riding is a pair of polished mudguards and a strip of chequered tape along the fuel tank. Fortunately, in between these two extremes are a large number of good trail bikes, in widely differing specifications, that will all give a good performance on the rough, either just as they come or with a few sage modifications.

In the next chapter, we will look at three widely differing machines and see how the features we have discussed so far are executed in practice.

One of the nicer Japanese trail bikes — the disc valved 125cc Kawasaki. This bike can be converted into a serious green lane machine with very little work

The perfect trail bike — the 'works' 250cc ISDT Jawa

The standard 125cc Suzuki as it left the factory in Japan

3 It takes all sorts

The three machines which we shall consider in this chapter are all genuine trail bikes. That is, they will meet the key criterion of Chapter 2, which was that the bike should function effectively on any terrain the rider wishes to cross. In the case of our three examples, they will go almost anywhere most trail riders will want to take a bike; however, their performance and intent is markedly different.

Firstly, let us look at one of the best 125cc trail bikes in production at present — the TS 125 Suzuki. This machine is a good example of Japanese mass-production engineering at its peak. Powered by a 125cc five-speed, two-stroke engine, the little Suzuki is quiet, easy to ride and extremely reliable. On the road, it has a cruising speed of 55mph with a few extra mph on top of that if, for some reason, one is in a hurry. In other words, the bike will perform well on the road and is a pleasant machine to use on short and medium length journeys on tarmac — quite suitable, in fact, for riding thirty or forty miles on normal roads to a chosen trail riding area.

Rough riding is hampered by gearing which is a little too high for the engine's power — particularly when the bike is ridden in a sedate manner by an inexperienced rider — and Japanese trials tyres which are hard work on slippery going. The low-slung exhaust system is also rather vulnerable to knocks.

Looking at the machine in more detail, it becomes apparent that the Suzuki has the basis for a sound trail bike. The wheels are the correct size — 21 inch front and 18 inch rear — the suspension is adequate at both ends and the riding position is satisfactory, if not ideal.

Looking at the first four points listed under General criteria, the Suzuki meets them all, and passes with confidence. The difficulties begin when one demands a better performance on the rough.

The most immediate problem is tyres, since the Japanese ones fitted as standard are too small in section, too hard in rubber compound and of the wrong shape. They need replacing with a suitable 'real' trials tyre, as previously outlined. There is no problem with the front and a 3.00 inch section trials tyre will fit beautifully. Unfortunately, the rear rim is narrower than that needed to carry a 4.00 inch tyre, and whilst it is possible to squeeze this big tyre on a narrow rim, (some weight conscious trials riders manage the job) a bigger WM3 section is better. Already, the price of a pair of tyres — but don't forget that the original Japanese ones can be sold to offset the cost — a rim and wheelbuilding has been rung up on the cash register.

The next task is to remove the front mudguard, which hugs the tyre and will become all too easily jammed with mud. This needs moving high up under the fork yokes and replacing with an unbreakable plastic item. Since you have a nice new mudguard at the front, it is just as well to remove the heavy lump of steel at the rear, which is prone to cracking and does not take kindly to being bashed against rocks.

After removing the mirrors and flashers, both of which Mother Nature will remove from your machine if you don't do the job yourself, and replacing the very slippery rubber covered footrests with steel loops, I would be tempted to leave the bike alone, for very quickly the law of diminishing returns will be invoked on the ever increasing expenditure.

As the bike stands at present, it will traverse most trails quite happily and little, if any, of its road virtues will be sacrificed. It still has full lights, a large and effective silencer and a fair turn of speed with good fuel economy. The next step is going to improve the bike's dirt performance immeasurably but it will also begin an increasingly firmer commitment to rough riding.

Because the Suzuki only produces some 12bhp, a low gearing must be used to maximize all the available power. On standard gearing, almost all trail riding would be done in first gear, with an occasional burst in second.

The front forks have been modified by the fitting of different springs and substituting a heavier oil for the damping. Note also that a high level plastic mudguard has been fitted and that the steel rims have been replaced by lightweight aluminium ones

The rear tyre is now a 4.00" x 18" Dunlop Trials tyre in place of the 3.25" x 18" Japanese original. The rear light is rubber mounted on a lightweight plastic mudguard

The standard Suzuki engine has been extensively modified to produce a power increase of 7 bhp. In doing this, petrol consumption has also been much increased

A larger rear sprocket, or smaller gearbox sprocket, will lower the overall gear ratios and make second and third gear useable on the trail with first as an emergency gear for tough hazards. The lower gearing also means that road speed will be reduced, and if the rider maintains a high speed, the engine will have to work much harder and a sharp drop in fuel consumption will be experienced. Now we have a real trail bike which is going to be much happier on rough going than it is on tarmac.

Further development is going to be both expensive and really only necessary if high speeds are envisaged on the rough. The front and rear suspension are excellent for normal sedate riding but can be improved for competition work. Gas filled Girling rear dampers, or Konis with Girling springs, are favoured by riders who race the TS 125s in enduros, but neither of these highly specialised units are cheap and their superiority over the standard Japanese damper will not be noticeable to the average rider out for a day's fun.

Similarly, the standard barrel can be 'ported' (ie having the various ports in the barrel re-cut for more power — an extremely skilled job and not to be undertaken by anyone other than a competent mechanic with access to accurate figures for port timing). Alternatively, the head and barrel assembly from the Suzuki TM motocrosser can be fitted. Either of these modifications will increase the power dramatically, but they will make the bike harder to ride and less pleasant as a plaything. They will also knock a substantial hole in the rider's wallet.

Assuming that your Suzuki's motor now gives sufficient power to be competitive in an enduro — and there are a number of such bikes around at present — it must be remembered that the crankshaft life, which after all, is a roadster item designed for 12bhp and not 18 or 20, will be reduced. Also the wear on the clutch and gearbox will be increased commensurately. In fact, the whole bike, including the cycle parts, will wear much faster than if it were left in standard trim. Further, there will be a sharp increase in the amount of maintenance required to keep the whole thing in good tune and performing effectively.

I have deliberately pursued this theme to the bitter end in order that two points be brought out in the open. Firstly, if you wish to compete in only one or two events a year — or more likely none at all — is it worth spending the money and time on modifying a machine in such a way that many of its original virtues of docility and sedateness will be reduced? In the crudest terms, do you need to own an expensive racing machine if you don't want to race?

Secondly, a TS 125 in full enduro trim, as we have outlined, will have almost doubled its original purchase price. Even then, the unpalatable fact is that the finished creation is still a modified roadster and has a number of faults which are inherent in a design of this type. The Suzuki happens to be an extremely good basic design — a classic amongst trail bikes — and so fares well, when modified. It would be possible to spend just as much time and money trying to convert one of the other 'road' trail bikes into competition trim and achieve nothing but disappointment and a series of nasty letters from your bank manager. If you find it necessary to improve a machine to this extent, then what you really need is a thoroughbred racing bike — one which is designed and intended for use in enduros. Such a machine will cost little more, (if anything at all) than our modified trail bike, but its standard performance, without any modifications, will be better than all but the very best professionally modified road machines.

There can be mitigating circumstances to this statement. For example, there is a lot of fun to be had from improving one's bike — I, for one, find this a very satisfying occupation. If the machine which is to form the basis of this modification can be obtained very cheaply, or if financial aid is available from a trade source, then these two are quite valid reasons for pursuing the theme, but on the whole, if you need, or more accurately WANT, a top-class sports trail bike, then the best option is to buy a specialised (and expensive) purpose-built machine.

The really intelligent rider is the one who knows whether he does want a bike such as this, or whether he would be far happier with something simpler and less trouble to own and ride. Remember, as we said in Chapter 2, if the bike satisfies you, then it is successful. This is the key to happiness on the trail.

Geoff Statham, press photographer and trail riding enthusiast, built just such a machine and whilst it has many faults, if viewed from a strictly technical viewpoint, it fits the rider's needs perfectly.

Three additional factors affected the bike in addition to the requirements we discussed previously. Firstly, the bike had to be cheap to build, because Geoff had heavy mortgage and family commitments. Secondly, it had to be a four-stroke — like many enthusiasts who are also traditionalists, two-strokes are anathema to Statham. Finally, because Geoff is of small stature, the bike had to be low and easily handled; a great big 650cc Triumph Metisse would not have been practical.

The basis of the bike is a frame and forks from a 1958 BSA B40 roadster and a 249cc C15 engine unit (again a BSA product) of the same vintage. The cycle parts are similar and Geoff could fit the engine, carefully re-built to trials specification with the correct cam and gearbox internals, into the frame without any problems.

Whilst an 18 inch rear wheel would have been ideal, a 19 inch one complete with a trials tyre became available cheaply and this was fitted along with a brand new 21 inch BSA Bantam front wheel. This wheel was very light and provided ample stopping power for the slow speeds that were envisaged.

C15 front forks give satisfactory, if not exemplary, handling and like so many of the bits used on this bike, were obtained very cheaply at a breaker's yard.

The same source provided a central oil tank, a Bultaco motocross petrol tank and various other bits and pieces. Only the lights, folding footrests and chain tensioner were purchased new. Ready to run, this very pleasant trail bike cost in the region of £50, to convert — plus the original roadster bits and pieces Geoff already had — a total of less than £100.

I rode the bike and was pleasantly surprised to find it handled well and would certainly tackle all but the most difficult trails. The short wheelbase and trials specification engine meant that it plonks along the tightest going at two or three miles an hour, in a very relaxed and effortless fashion. The four-stroke engine was tractable and provided ample bottom-end power for most occasions.

Geoff Statham, proud owner of this C15-engined trail bike. This BSA provides an attractive and interesting change when most trail bikes are Japanese two-strokes. Although a fifteen year old design, the C15 was quite able to cope with most trails

In deference to the engine's age, and the low overall gearing, Geoff cruises his BSA at around 45mph, with perhaps another 10mph in reserve. Regardless of how the bike is used, it returns 85mpg, which means that one tank full of petrol will last for a whole day's trail riding. In fact, it completely meets its owner's requirements.

What the BSA will not do is travel very quickly across rough country. Immediately one starts to drive it hard, the inadequacies of the front suspension become apparent, as does the very short wheelbase and the engine's lack of out and out power. But the vitally important thing is that the bike does what Geoff wants it to do — a point which cannot be re-iterated too often. Statham has never ridden in an enduro and has no particular wish to. This being the case, his motorcycle functions in a perfectly adequate manner and what is more pertinent, his whole machine has cost less than many competition orientated riders will pay for a new front wheel.

The lesson to be learnt from Geoff Statham's machine is to know what you want from your trail bike; build or buy the bike which meets your requirements at the most sensible price, and don't be persuaded by the pundits who try to criticise your choice because it doesn't meet **their** requirements and standards.

Top left *Folding footrests were a worthwhile modification*
Top right *The C15 was very quiet, even with this tiny silencer. A low noise level is of paramount importance if free access to trails is to be assured in the future*
Middle left *Small, well-protected lights are fitted since the bike is used mainly on the rough*
Middle right *The power plant is basically a C15 trials motor. An air-filter is normally fitted but was undergoing repair when this photograph was taken*
Bottom left *The whole bike is neat and uncluttered — showing a sound awareness of what makes a good trail bike*

A motorcycle which does meet the most rigid demands of the trail riding afficienado is the 175cc KTM. In ten years of track testing competition motorcycles, this little KTM stands out as being one of the outstanding machines.

I had it on loan from Comerfords, the British KTM importers, and wrote a very favourable report in the American magazine, *Cycle Illustrated.* It had a top speed approaching 90mph, acceleration which would have kept it competitive in a motocross meeting, six speed gearbox, magnesium engine and hubs and a whole host of high quality appendages designed to make the bike a winner in competition.

Thanks to Comerfords liberal road testing policy, I had the bike on loan for some months and after slogging away at a typewriter for five or six hours, I would take the KTM out of the garage and go howling off around the country lanes, blowing away the cobwebs. Because the engine was a highly tuned competition unit, it did not function effectively until it was revving freely. Thus it was best kept screaming most of the time to make full use of the bike's potential. Experimenting with the six speed gearbox, and keeping the throttle well open, it was possible to have great fun playing racers.

For me, this was ideal. When I first rode the KTM, I had ten years' motocross experience to draw on. The majority of the time I spent playing with the KTM was either in deserted lanes, miles from the nearest house, or on my friend's farm — a venue which normally hosts full-blooded motocross machines. In other words, I had sufficient skill to ride the KTM as it was intended and fortunately, the facilities to enjoy the bike without causing offence to the general public.

The KTM provided a challenge to my skill as a rider and gave exhilarating rewards in return if these challenges were met. It was not an easy bike to ride, but in mastering its difficulties one could travel very quickly across the roughest ground and at a sustained pace which would have wrecked most other machines. These traits put to practice in an enduro would mean a good chance of winning an award, or class, or whatever else the rider was capable of.

To trained eyes, the KTM possesses a functional beauty all its own

In design, the KTM had all the features one would expect to find on a thoroughbred racing machine. The wheels were 21 inch front and 18 inch rear — as we would expect — but the wheel rims were aluminium and hubs magnesium alloy — both vital and very expensive weight saving measures. The front suspension, manufactured for KTM by the world-renowned Ceriani concern, was of motocross origin, whilst the rear was of motocross design, and aimed at giving a long travel to the rear wheel by mounting the dampers well-forward of the wheel spindle.

The engine was a huge finned two-stroke, with a host of international successes to its credit, and featuring every conceivable modification to improve both power and reliability. Unfortunately, the large fins resonated badly and at low speeds; the rider was continually aware of the irritating drone from the motor.

So we could go on, listing the KTM's excellent design features and eulogising on its high-speed virtues. The KTM is good at the job it was intended to do — that is, win enduros. The Austrian designers never built the bike with the intention that it should spend half its life pottering along the trails at only a few miles an hour and sure enough, the bike rebels, if treated in this manner. It revolts by oiling plugs, making the rider aware of all sorts of whirrs, clanks, grumbles and groans, which in the heat of competition he never notices, and by generally indicating that the throttle should be opened and the racing commenced.

Although only having a swept volume of 175cc, the KTM is capable of over 85 mph. The engine has large, coarse finning so that it runs cool under the most arduous conditions. The sidecases are magnesium in order to save weight. In fact, every inch a racing machine

At the rear, long travel suspension helps the handling. Note the stout chainguard and magnesium rear brake plate. All very sophisticated but also expensive, particularly if the rider will derive no benefit from these luxuries

Jumping downhill is no problem — just open the throttle and the front end will rise. Would you find this fun, or would you prefer a more sedate style of riding?

The KTM is a racing bike and is at its best when driven flat out. It is not happy pottering along quietly

The KTM is one of the biggest bargains in its class, since its price in no way reflects the quality and sophistication of the design. Yet even so, it is possible to buy a small Japanese trail bike, a machine like that belonging to Geoff Statham, and a moped for commuting, for about the same price that a KTM will cost. The unpalatable fact of the matter is that it is impossible to produce an exotic hand-built motorcycle, using expensive alloys, and with a lavish specification, at a price equal to that of a mass-produced machine. Only a fool would expect otherwise.

What the KTM offers is the chance to own a thoroughbred racing machine, capable of winning. However, like all thoroughbreds, it must be treated with respect. It is little use owning a Rolls-Royce and then complaining about the price of petrol. Similarly, if you object to the high rate of wear knobbly tyres always show when used on the tarmac, or the maintenance required to keep the KTM in top tune or even the gallon of two-stroke mixture the bike will consume every 35 miles when driven hard, then you should not be a KTM owner.

THE KTM is what I personally want from a trail bike, and had I not been doing development work for Fantic Motor at the time, I would undoubtedly have bought one. After so long looking to the needs of motocross machines, the work that the KTM would require is child's play. Since 75% of all my trail riding is competitive riding, or practising riding for enduros, the KTM suits my needs ideally and the slow speed irritations are more than worth suffering in return for the chance of going very quickly, when necessary. Finally, I would derive great pleasure from owning an exotic and sophisiticated motorcycle, and I would acknowledge this by not grumbling about the price tag. In other words, the KTM would meet my needs for trail riding, and since these needs are complex and demanding, I must be prepared to pay the price in terms of initial cost, maintenance, running costs and the challenge the bike will make on my riding skills.

In this Chapter, we have looked at three widely differing motorcycles and seen how their specifications and design interpret the needs of the trail motorcycle. From these three random examples — and we could have looked at another 12 or 15 permutations of differing marques and arrived at the same overall picture — it may be seen that once the basic criteria for a trail machine have been achieved, it is very much up to the individual rider's needs to dictate the bike he wants to own.

I have gone to great lengths to stress this because trail riding is the only branch of motorcycling where there really is a wide choice regarding machines. A trail rider can be happy with whatever makes him happy, unlike a road racer, for instance, who would only be satisfied with a pukka racer, or a trials rider who needs an out and out trials iron. Please remember that it is not the bike which satisfies the sage journalist which you should aim for, or the one which Joe Cool rides around the paddock of the big international road race meeting, but the bike which does what you want and expect a trail bike to do — no more and no less.

Light weight and fierce power mean that the front end will rise easily. This is a great help to the experienced rider but might prove an embarrassment to a beginner

4 Buying a bike

Now that we have discussed trail bikes in general terms and examined some specific examples, you will probably have some idea of the kind of bike you wish to own. Because there is such a wide spread in the trail bike spectrum, it would be impossible to formulate a set of rules for purchasing every single type of machine. Instead, I propose to base my comments on a mythical average machine which might well approximate to the TS 125 Suzuki, modified as suggested in Chapter 3. That is, not a full-blown racing machine, but a genuine trail bike intended to perform at its best on the rough. Many of the comments echo those I made on buying a motocross bike, in *Ride it! The Complete Book of Motocross,* and I make no apology for this. Purchasing a trail bike and buying a motocrosser have much in common, and the new-comer to off-road riding could do much worse than take along an experienced racer when he is buying a machine — particularly a second-hand one — since racers tend to be both aware in the mechanical sense and also tight-fisted when it comes to bargain hunting.

Every newcomer must make two basic and important choices about machines before he can start riding. Firstly, he must decide to buy new or second-hand machinery and secondly, whether to purchase privately or through a dealer. In general terms, it is best to avoid a machine which has been owned by a very inexperienced rider, who has used the bike regularly for trail riding. Such bikes are often kept running merely by their owner's enthusiasm, with scant regard for serious and regular maintenance. Trail bikes need much love and attention if they are to be kept in good health and this sort of care tends to come from riders who have found the need for regular spanner-work the hard way.

However, if you can find a bike which has done little actual cross-country work, possibly because the owner was none too adventurous, and the engine/gearbox unit is in good condition, then this should make a good buy since the cycle parts will not have suffered from overwork. In this case, the bike is likely to be in better condition, because road-work is not nearly so demanding and therefore maintenance is not so critical.

On occasions, ex-works machines (ie, bikes which have once belonged to a factory race or development department) come up for sale. These bikes seem to have a fascination for motorcyclists in all branches of the sport, and trail riding is no exception. The thought of actually owning a bike which has just won a medal in the ISDT is very attractive, as is the thought of riding a bike with a one-off special frame.

Occasionally, these bikes can make a good buy for the private owner. For example, if the machine offered for sale is a specially prepared version of a production machine. Then a good buy can be had IF, and only if, you really want a racing machine.

In other cases, it is worth thinking about the wider aspects of your purchase before parting with that pile of pound notes. Now that you own a Massambula Gold Medal Special, where (other than the Massambula factory in Zululand) do you go for spare parts? Fitting a set of piston rings might be straightforward enough but how about shimming the gearbox mainshaft and getting the information to do the job, particularly if you don't speak fluent Zulu? Finally, it is worth remembering that factory machines are supremely disposable and once the current model has been superseded then not only will what few spare parts that are left over from factory competition be quickly used up but the parent racing shop will soon lose interest.

Owning a rare and exotic machine can be a hobby in itself. I keep an ex-works BSA motocross machine for this reason and it gives me a great deal of pleasure. By the same token, I also have to keep a mountain of special bits for it and a vital list of telephone numbers of people who know about the racing BSAs. Fortunately, because there were a lot of factory BSAs around for a long period, there are a commensurate number of experts who are usually willing to help.

Taken in this sense, owning a 'special' is a lot of fun, but not, I would think, a practical proposition for someone who wants to ride regularly and in the process, wear it out. The more mundane production machines might be less attractive at first sight, but they are infinitely more practical for most riders.

The question of new or second-hand is something of a vexing one. One school of thought argues that only a new bike will give a rider any indication of his abilities whilst at the other end of the spectrum, there is a group of worthies insisting that any sort of bike will do for the novice since he will wreck it in any case.

My opinion falls between the two extremes, erring perhaps towards the ride a wreck theory. Having said this, let me say that I would never advise any rider, regardless of experience, to purchase a really worn out bike, since he will inherit nothing but heartache and expense — neither of which is conducive to happy riding.

Almost all new bikes are sold through dealers, and if you use this method of attack, you will be relieved of having to make the choice of buying from the trade or privately. In either case, *Caveat Emptor* (let the buyer beware) is the rule to memorise and obey implicitly.

Trail bikes inevitably have a hard life and the great majority of second-hand machines are sold without guarantee. This means that the purchaser, and no-one else, is responsible for assessing the value of the machine. In practice, if you buy from a reputable dealer, he will usually make some sort of statement about the bike and then back his assessment with after-sales service. For example, you might discover that the big end was in poor condition after stripping the motor at home, and depending on the price paid for the bike, the dealer might offer you discount on a new bearing or perhaps a free replacement. It must be remembered that with the cheaper trail bikes the dealer will, in all probability, sell the machine just as it stands, so don't expect him to re-build it for you if it was bought at bargain basement prices in the first place.

If you choose to buy privately, then you are really on your own in the big, wide world. It is most certainly true that remarkable bargains can be had in the private sector, but it is also true that such forays can be disastrous — particularly for the novice.

The important thing to remember is not to rush into buying a bike merely to have something — anything — on which to ride. I have given in to the lust for new machinery on several occasions and the penalties for weakness can be heavy in view of the cost of modern trail bikes, even second-hand ones, and the percentage rate on finance loans.

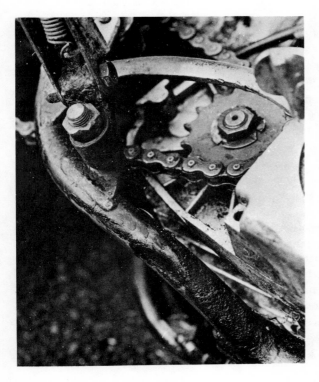

A minor dent in a frame tube, such as this one, is no great detriment. However, be wary of any damage to the footrest mount itself

One's first move is to ascertain who has owned the bike in the past, particularly establishing what sort of approach the rider has had towards his sport. The ideal bike to buy is one which has been owned by an experienced trail rider who is basically non-competitive in his riding, since he will invariably have had sufficient experience to maintain it properly and yet it will not have been used to its full extent on most occasions.

Before we discuss some of the criteria to be employed when choosing a second-hand machine, it is as well to point out that the greatest single source of bargains in the whole rough riding world is: last year's models.

Careful scanning of the trade papers sometime after Christmas will reveal that the majority of importers sell off their old stock at this time, in order to make space in the showroom for the new season's models. In many cases, there will be only superficial differences between the new bike and its predecessor, and yet really healthy discounts can be obtained — particularly if there is no part-exchange of your old bike involved in the deal. If you can find a marque with a good reputation, and preferably one whose latest model is almost identical to the previous one, then purchasing last year's bike can be a way of getting a new and competitive machine at second-hand prices.

Try to choose a machine which is fairly popular and well known, preferably with a dealer in your area with a good stock of spares. Avoid the very esoteric brands which are sold in small quantities, unless there is some mitigating circumstance. For example, if your next door neighbour has a sponsored ride on a Mud Plugger de luxe in enduros, then it is a fair reason for buying one of these rare brands, because he is in a position to be able to supply spares and specialised knowledge. Of course, he may not like you, in which case your best bet is to try and beat him often enough to impress the Mud Plugger management and steal his works ride.

Having decided on a suitable bike, the next step is to locate its whereabouts. This is usually done through the classified advertisements in the motorcycle press and by indulging in half a dozen phone calls to major competition dealers, who will normally have the best selection of trail bikes. These resources will also reveal the average price for a given type of bike, and will give you some idea of what to aim for in your negotiations.

Take a knowledgeable friend along with you; this is essential. If your mate is not knowledgeable, then at least he can hold your hand and nod knowingly. Then go through the following checklist, slowly and thoroughly, remembering a derivative of the old adage "Buy in haste, repent over the next two years' finance repayments".

General

1   Is the bike clean and tidy? Is it obviously well-cared for?
2   Are any modifications neat and workmanlike? Beware if they make the bike abnormally non-standard.
3   On a four-stroke, is the oil clean? (Remember, with an oil bearing frame, it is difficult to keep the oil spotlessly clean, even if it is fresh. However, be warned by obviously filthy lubricant.)
4   Is the air-filter clean?
5   Are the nuts rounded?
6   Are the cables frayed?
7   Are there any bonuses with the bike? (eg, spares, clothing)
8   Is the vendor willing to give a guarantee with the machine?

A point to remember about this section is that you are assessing the machine in general terms to determine whether it has been well looked after. The state of the air-filter element is an almost certain indicator of the engine's condition since poor air-filtration will wreck a motor in no time at all. A dirty filter also reflects a poor attitude on the part of the rider and points to other aspects of inadequate maintenance.

To clinch a deal, it is common practice for a dealer to make some concession regarding spares, and it might also be possible to purchase some special tools along with the selling price of the bike. If the rider is retiring, he might also be prepared to extend the deal to some clothing as well — something the budget trail rider should bear in mind.

Having established that the bike is worth investigating further, go through the next check list, which will give you a fair idea of its mechanical state.

Mechanical check list

1   Will the engine start easily? (nb. beware of a bike "which hasn't been run for a bit so it's a devil to start", or "it normally starts first kick, it must be the weather". A good engine should start on the kickstart without too much trouble. Remember, if the bike won't start in the comfort of its owner's garage, you can hold scant hope that it will fire whilst immersed in three feet of ooze.
2   Does the engine sound crisp and healthy?

Checking wheel bearings for excessive wear

3   Are there any obvious clankings or other dubious noises?
4   Now the engine has been run, are there any oil leaks?
5   Is the front fork action smooth and easy? If it isn't, check that the fork legs are not twisted or bent. If they are twisted in the yokes, this can easily be remedied by slackening off the pinch bolts and realigning by pulling at the handlebar, but bends in the fork stanchions are more or less permanent and tend to be expensive.
6   Do the rear suspension units clank on rebound? If they do, this usually indicates that the damping has failed.
7   Are the wheels true and the spokes unbroken? Most trail bike wheels will be buckled to some degree, so don't worry about the odd ¼ inch inaccuracy. Concern yourself with large flats, which show something has been hit hard.
8   Do the brakes stop the wheels smoothly, and without noise?
9   Are the wheel bearings obviously worn? Check this by rocking the wheel to and fro at 90° to the direction of rotation.
10   Check the seams on the frame. Have any of them been re-welded?
11   Have the footrest mounts been bent? Link with question number five to build up a picture of whether or not the bike has been dropped heavily.

Questions 1, 2 and 3 will indicate the condition of the engine in general terms. If it starts easily and sounds healthy then it is almost a certainty that it will produce ample power for the beginner. Two things are worth noting. Firstly, the straight cut gears employed on many two-stroke engines nowadays, particularly those with a competition bias, make rather a lot of noise but you will be listening for discordant noises coming from some bearing not in harmony with its fellow. Also, most two-strokes produce clouds of blue smoke when they are first started, Don't be put off by this unless it persists for some considerable time.

The sections appertaining to suspension are quite important, since both front and rear shocks really have to work in cross-country riding. Most rear dampers have what is known as a 50/50 action, which means that there is compression both on compression and rebound. It is difficult to tell whether there is damping on compression, but if it is lacking on the rebound, then it is fair to assume that it isn't there on the compression either.

Questions 5, 9 and 10 should be linked together in your mind, so that a picture of whether or not the bike is really bent can be formed. To bend a footrest mount is difficult, so look for damage to the sub-frame and bottom engine rail. If the frame has been re-welded, other than to facilitate some sensible modification, question the owner as to why this was necessary. Beware of a bike which shows signs of repeated cycle repairs: you will stand a good chance of becoming a proficient welder with such a machine.

5 Trail bike to enduro racer

Let me begin by saying that this Chapter is not an exercise to urge you to buy a TS 250 Suzuki trail bike and begin modifying it. Nor is it an attempt to persuade you to rush off to Eddie Crooks' shop at Barrow-in-Furness and buy a replica of the machine which is described in this Chapter.

What I wanted to do was to take a standard trail bike — preferably a Japanese one because they proliferate the countryside in such great numbers — and develop it for green lane riding so that each modification could be related to a purpose and then demonstrated in practical terms.

However, whilst this seemed a good idea to me, the various importers threw up their hands in horror at the thought of one of their machines being changed in any shape, way or form. I munificently put this down to their pure and untarnished belief that what their parent factories supplied was perfect in every shape, way or form.

Thus, the idea was shelved, until one day, in conversation with my long-time friend and sometime sponsor, Eddie Crooks, we got around to discussing the then brand new Suzuki trail bike, the TS 250A. Although at the time I had never seen the bike, when Eddie suggested it might be the basis for an enduro machine, I was most interested, for in addition to being a first class road racer, Crooks has also won more than one medal in the ISDT.

I had already carried out development work for Eddie and when it was suggested that I might like to develop the TS 250A for enduro work I was delighted, for not only could my original aim of writing this Chapter be achieved, but once again I would be working with one of the most knowledgeable and enthusiastic dealers in Britain — a fact which pleased me immensely. Also, I would be involved in developing a brand new bike and this prospect excites me as much as riding.

Apart from having a genuine interest in every facet of motorcycle sport — often where there is no commercial advantage to be gained — Crooks had another reason for sponsoring this project. Many of his customers wanted a trail bike which would cope with severe going — certainly something more esoteric in design than the Suzuki had to offer at the time — but were frightened by the rather high prices of the competition thoroughbreds and also their somewhat unforgiving nature in the hands of amateurs. Would it be possible to provide an economically priced alternative to the pukka enduro bikes and yet still produce a bike which would deal with any sort of trail, regardless of how tough, and provide a reasonably competitive ride in enduros? It was an interesting challenge, and one which whetted my appetite.

Thus a Suzuki came to be the choice for this Chapter. But the exercise can be undertaken with any trail bike, Japanese or European, providing it meets certain basic requirements. We were exceptionally fortunate in that the Suzuki turned out to be a Cinderella in chromium-plated rags. A few waves of the magic spanner, and the results were more pleasing than we had dared hope. However, whatever the bike, much improvement can be made by following the basic pattern I used to modify the Suzuki. There will be detail differences, obviously, but the scenario will be much the same.

If we look back to Chapter 2, there were four criteria for judging the suitability of a bike for trail riding. The first and second referred to the engine; ease of starting, tractability and reliability were mentioned. The third referred to ground clearance and the fourth to engine noise. The sensible — the essential — thing to do before beginning any modification to an existing machine is to ask yourself, "Is this really going to be worth all the trouble, or would I be better advised to choose more suitable basic material?"

On two occasions in the last six years, when I have been approached by importers to carry out development work on cross-country machines, I have declined after a short test ride. The last time this happened, I wrote back

The standard TS 250 Suzuki

to the sales manager who was responsible for the project, and said, "Dear Herbie, your latest Bonga Wonga special is so far behind the competition that if we worked hard on it for six months, it would only be as good as a standard 250 Gizzly and the production versions would still be just as bad. Wouldn't you be better going back to the drawing board and having another go from scratch?"

Obviously I wasn't alone in my opinion, because they did.

An old maxim from the road racing world holds good for trail bikes as well. That is, you can make a poor bike fair, a fair bike good, and a good bike excellent but there is no way that you can make a poor bike excellent or a good bike into a world-beater. Even with infinite talent, there is only so much that can be done with the basic material.

In choosing the Suzuki, we had a good basis for the project. The engine is derived from the TM motocross unit and has an excellent reputation for reliability. Like all Japanese bikes, it starts well and is quiet. As for the cycle parts, they look basically right and there are particularly pleasing features such as the high level silencer, sensibly tucked in so that it does not interfere with riding in the standing position, and the long-travel motocross type front suspension.

A quick road test confirmed my opinion. The bike was basically right. The motor pulled well and was responsive and the bike handled easily — just the sort of characteristics needed for an enduro machine. Happy that there was a future in the machine, work commenced.

The first job was to relieve the bike of all its weight, in the form of road orientated accessories, and also to reduce the number of things which could be a possible source of trouble in adverse conditions.

The most obvious target was the steel mudguards which, as well as being extremely heavy, are also likely to get badly damaged the first time they come into contact with a tree or rock. They were removed and replaced by a Preston Petty Big Mudder motocross mudguard on the front, and an enduro unit, incorporating a tail light, at the rear. I specifically recommend this brand not because I am receiving a retainer (although always open to offers) but because in my experience, they are by far the best in the world and will withstand an immense amount of abuse.

Plastic mudguards are both lighter than steel and far more resistant to damage

The best types are Preston Petty Big Mudder
motocross front mudguards and an enduro unit
from the same firm for the rear, which incorporates
a neat tail light. Note that the mudguard is mounted
high beneath the fork yoke, motocross style, so
that it does not clog with mud. Front light is a
7 inch Aprilla whose main virtues are low cost
and light weight but certainly not lighting power

The Preston Petty enduro rear mudguard

The front mudguard is mounted high, as on a motocross machine, so that it will never clog with mud. On the Suzuki, the yoke is already tapped to take four 8mm bolts, so fixing is very easy, but there should be no problem on any bike. If you are new to competition work, it is perhaps worth taping the mudguard in place first and then checking the frame clearance, rather than drilling holes and then discovering a miscalculation when it is too late to correct. To do the job properly, the fork springs should be removed so that the sliders can be moved upwards to their maximum extent, so permitting the wheel to come right up to the frame.

Now the fun can really begin. The Suzuki in standard trim carries all the paraphenalia of a lavishly equipped road machine — a whole load of beautifully designed and heavy equipment which is totally useless on a cross-country machine.

How much is removed depends largely on what you want to do with the bike. The final rôle of the Suzuki was to be a racing machine, so stripping was down to the bare bone — a state which I would recommend for a serious trail bike.

Off came the indicators, lights, horn, tachometer, steering lock and ignition switch, along with the battery and associated brackets. On the floor of the workshop grew a pile of new and unused, very expensive Suzuki parts. If the bike has been purchased new, and from a Suzuki dealer with a sporting background, it is likely that he may give you an allowance for the spares removed, against the Preston Petty mudguards or knobbly tyres, or alternatively they can be sold easily through the classified advertisements in the weekly motorcycle press. Do take care of them, for they are your passport to a cheap conversion.

Most trail bikes have ignition systems which can be wired to run independently of the battery and the first job in the reconstruction — taking bits off is easy and fun, putting new and better ones in their place is much harder, but still lots of fun — is to wire the ignition direct. That is, as soon as the bike is kicked over, it will start without any ignition switch being operated. This means that there is no switch malfunction and the ignition system can be both simplified and more adequately waterproofed and protected against the other vagaries of a wet, rocky trail in the middle of winter. What MUST be done at the same time is to fit a reliable ignition cut-out, for there has just got to be some way of stopping the engine if the throttle sticks open, or a carburettor slide jams, otherwise the consequences could be very severe indeed.

The Suzuki has a rocker-type cut out switch incorporated in the throttle drum which I didn't like at all. It has a habit of knocking itself off at the most inopportune moments and perversely, did not work on the one occasion when I really needed it. I am loth to criticise the original design because it was really not designed to be abused in the way I treated it. Nevertheless, I felt much happier when I had fitted a simple Miller cut-out button, which now rests under my right thumb, for use in dire emergencies. The Miller switch is simple in design, but when sealed against water, works every time and as such may stand as example for all enduro equipment. Keep it simple, and the chances of failure are considerably reduced.

A working example of this theme is the removal of the electric horn. An electric horn requires wiring, a switch, and current to function — three items which are all susceptible to failure. Remove them all and put in their place a simple bulb horn which meets the law's demands, and three more problems immediately disappear.

Having discarded the Suzuki's superb lights, units well worthy of any long-distance touring machine, some replacement was necessary since it is often essential to have some form of lights, even on an enduro machine, (in fact in some events, lights are obligatory) and every trail bike should have the ability to travel a few miles along public roads after dark. Like the horn, we are thinking of the minimum legally necessary and not superb lighthouses with which to illuminate the trail at midnight. Rather, a reserve measure to enable the rider to finish off the day's riding in safety, without fear of running foul of a vigilant rural bobby.

One of the most suitable lighting kits easily available is that supplied as an optional extra on the Montesa trials bikes. This consists of a 5 inch headlamp, all the associated switchgear, and rear lamp, which is of no value since the Preston Petty enduro rear mudguard contains a much better integral rear lamp unit.

The wiring is straightforward and the switchgear also contains a cut-out button and an electric horn switch, the wiring for which I removed on the grounds that two less wires are two less to cause trouble.

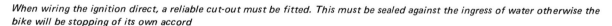

When wiring the ignition direct, a reliable cut-out must be fitted. This must be sealed against the ingress of water otherwise the bike will be stopping of its own accord

I find that it is a good idea to spray the inside of the switch and headlamp with Rocol Rust Shield, a lanolin-based rust inhibitor. Do take care not to spray the reflector in the headlamp, otherwise what little lighting power there is will be lost. The lighting equipment is made by Aprilla, in Italy, and is of poor quality, though adequate for the job. A coating of Rust Shield stops everything from rusting away.

Having removed the battery, a problem now occurs in how to dissipate the voltage from the powerful flywheel generator. Again, this is not a difficulty exclusive to Suzuki, but to any bike where the generator normally feeds the battery and where the current is then fed directly to the lights. In practical terms, the bulbs blow every time the engine revs. and the current rises above 6 volts.

The correct way to deal with this is to fit a Lucas Clipper Diode in the circuit, which will convert the excess current into heat. Unfortunately, although these clever little gadgets appear in the Lucas catalogue, they are almost impossible to obtain — even with access to the right sources within the trade — and when one can be found, they tend not to be too reliable.

Fortunately, like most trail bikes, the Suzuki generates 6 volt current. This is because a 12 volt battery is just too bulky and heavy to be easily housed in a small capacity machine, particularly when weight is such an important criterion. This means that a 12 volt bulb fitted to the front headlamp will effectively absorb any voltage surge produced by the generator at high revs. I used a 35 watt bulb normally fitted to a Honda four, and whilst the light emitted at very low revs. is more a bright yellow than white, it is quite satisfactory once the engine is working normally. Two 6 volt festoon bulbs are fitted to the rear lamp in the normal way and work quite happily. In many hours of riding, the system has functioned perfectly and the light, when needed, is certainly legal and no worse than some purpose built lighting sets I have seen in use. Best of all, it is simple, with one switch for on and one for dip, with no diodes, transistors, resistors or anything to go wrong. Simplicate, not complicate, should be the aim for every trail rider.

My personal preference is for the speedometer to be offset, so that an air-bottle can be carried on the cross-brace of the handlebars, without obscuring the rider's view. Some riders like to tuck it away directly over the steering head, behind the handlebars; the site is a matter for the individual. However, wherever it finally does come to rest, the speedometer must be well-protected from over-hanging tree branches, or possible damage if the bike is dropped.

The final modification in this initial stage was to fit a pair of MotoPlat lever shrouds, which are a tremendous help in preventing the ingress of water into the front brake and clutch cables.

Motoplas lever shrouds keep much of the dirt and water out of the cables

At this stage, many riders will wish to cease work, for the bike is an excellent compromise. Still using the initial road gearing, which is quite suitable for all but the most severe trails, the bike will cruise happily at 70mph and still return in excess of 65mpg. The trials tyres handle very well on tarmac, and, if some respect is shown, are adequate for the rough. With the addition of plastic mudguards, well-protected lighting set and the work undertaken to both lighten the machine and increase its reliability, the performance of the bike will be enhanced on both the road and the rough. If I were not competition minded, then this is the sort of thing which I would be looking for. Ideal for following an observed trial as a spectator, equally at home as a commuter machine, and capable of both a day's green lane riding and a trip to the seaside in summer.

After the basic modifications the Suzuki performed admirably and might well satisfy your requirements. Before progressing further, ask yourself if the extra money and effort involved will be repaid by achieving the type of riding which YOU want to do

As we noted earlier, have the intelligence to recognise what you want YOUR motorcycle to do and then build it accordingly, and do not be swayed by what afficionados or advertising men insist that you want.

Noting my own advice, and remembering my initial brief from Eddie Crooks, the Suzuki as it stood did not satisfy me. It could be made to go, and steer, markedly better, and this was the next step.

So far, it should have been possible to carry out all the modifications without any additional outlay over the bike's original purchase price, that is, assuming it is new, or at least off-set the cost considerably by selling the second-hand parts privately. From now on, costs begin to mount.

The latest Suzukis have the push-pull Mikuni carburettor, with positive closing of the throttle slide by cable, instead of relying just on the slide return spring. This carburettor supposedly gives cleaner combustion — in answer to the ever increasing plethora of American anti-legislation — but it is inferior in two respects for a competition carburettor. First, there are effectively two cables (in practice one big one with two leads back to the throttle drum) and two cables, added to the one which operates the Posi-Force oil feed, makes three. Three cables mean treble trouble on an enduro bike. Also, the cable looks as if it would be a three and a half year job to change, and certainly not the sort of task to be undertaken on the top of a Welsh mountain, with frozen fingers and time running out very rapidly. Yet again, reduce the number of things to go wrong and the opportunities for trouble are also reduced.

For some reason best known to Mikuni, the new carburettor gives a rather woolly performance, and when we substituted a competition carburettor, of the same make, normally used on the 325cc Bultaco Trials bike, the improvement was most noticeable. Not only was the engine much crisper, and far more willing to rev., but it was also extremely responsive at low revs. and under load, just the sort of conditions to be found in enduros.

In this case a carburettor change was a universal panacea but please remember to think before laying your money on the spares' counter. I have been riding and modifying competition machines for twelve years and even so I could not have chosen the correct alternative carburettor for the brand new bike at the first attempt. What was needed was the specialist knowledge of Eddie's race mechanic, John Wren, who spends five days of each week working with Mikuni carburettors and Suzuki motorcycles. With this sort of intensive experience of one carburettor type and one marque, it is possible to make very accurate predictions — consequently we got it right first time, even to the extent of choosing the correct main jet.

Performance is much improved by substituting a competition Mikuni for the standard 'anti-pollution' device. BEFORE spending any money on a new carburettor, check with an acknowledged expert for your marque, preferably one who races a bike in enduros or motocross

I was working with a Suzuki and therefore went to a Suzuki expert. A sensible rider will do the same, for whichever motorcycle he is developing. In addition to the Mikuni, Dell O'rto's VHB is another excellent unit which can improve an engine almost beyond recognition. Another good carburettor is the Amal Mark 2 and although not particularly competition minded, the Amal technical staff in Birmingham are most co-operative regarding advice.

Firstly, think what you intend to achieve with the carburettor change. Then consult with the experts who are familiar with your bike and let them suggest a carburettor. Then check with the carburettor experts. Finally, if you are happy that a new carburettor will achieve what you want, buy it. Following this system, not only will your bank balance stay healthy, or relatively so, but the end result of your planning is far more likely to be effective.

These rules are just as effective for any modification, whether it is the new chromium plated piston or works replica cylinder head. Think, plan and check BEFORE modifying, rather than try to rectify the mistakes afterwards.

In addition to fitting the Mikuni, I also cut off the spark arrestor in the tip of the Suzuki's silencer. This is fitted to meet US regulations and serves no useful purpose in Britain. It also clogs with carbon very quickly, reducing performance even more. The engine breathes more freely and the noise level is increased only marginally (although the bike is still one of the quietest 250s).

This modification can be usefully carried out on all trail bikes which have American specifications. A warning note should be sounded in that whilst removing the spark arrestor is quite permissible, the silencer itself should never be altered in any way. Modern two-strokes depend largely on the silencer design for their power and fuel economy since without the scavenging effect of the expansion chamber, (which is really what a silencer is, in disguise) the two-stroke engine would be most wasteful. Designing an expansion chamber, particularly one which is also a silencer, is a job for a creative engineer and a large computer. The shape has to be constructed so that the engine's natural resonances are made to act as an extractor and often the dimensions for a given engine might be critical to a ¼ inch. Obviously, even the most gifted amateur mechanic is going to have scant chance of improving the design merely by attacking it with a hacksaw or large drill. If I can re-inforce this even further by saying that I know many professional tuners — men who are really talented with engines — and they alter the shape or size of a two-stroke engine's expansion only with great reluctance and extreme care. And in most cases, the reason for the alteration is to fit an existing engine into a new chassis where the original design could not be accommodated. The best that they can hope for is parity with the original design.

With the addition of the new carburettor, and the modified silencer, the Suzuki will reach almost 90mph on the original road-gearing, and will pull hard from zero revs. Unfortunately, for some reason best known to themselves, Suzuki made first gear in this engine very high, so that whilst the motor's excellent pulling power will permit road-gearing to be used for trail riding, the ultra-hard going of an enduro requires a really low bottom gear. In this case, a compromise has to be reached, for the overall gearing must still be high enough to allow high speeds in the forestry sections, where much time can be made up if the bike has a good top speed. Also, I like to be able to rest the motor on such sections by using a high gear at medium revs, rather than screaming it to destruction.

We played about with various options and decided on using a 15t gearbox sprocket with the standard size rear sprocket. This gives a top gear high enough for 75mph, and a pleasant cruising speed of 65mph, with a little bit left in reserve if I am in a very brave mood. But first gear would still be too high, were it not for the Suzuki's remarkable pulling power. The engine is now so responsive that it will pull hard from a thousand rpm, which means that all but the most severe hazard can be negotiated without resort to clutch slipping.

This is fine if the engine you are working with is as flexible as the Suzuki's but if it is not, you must err on the side of a low first gear, for there is little use being able to roar along forestry tracks in true ISDT style, only to get stuck in the first stream bed the course crosses.

Even if the bike is not being used for enduros, but just for very serious trail riding, the same maxim applies — there must be an emergency lifeline for use on that ten yards of killer going, whether it be rocks, mud or a savage camber, which would otherwise call a halt to the proceedings.

If you really want the best of both worlds, the latest 6 speed Jawa ISDT bikes will reach over 100mph on the rough and still manage to climb up a sheer rock wall in first gear, which just proves that it is possible to provide the perfect machine for the job, with unlimited skill, money and facilities. Unfortunately, most of us lesser mortals are unlikely even to sit on such a bike, and the chances of racing one are very remote. Still, we can live in hope.

At this stage I must digress slightly to mention another one of the Suzuki's virtues which would cause problems if it were absent; that is, fuel consumption, or rather, lack of it. Driven flat out during testing sessions, with two riders sharing the work and therefore able to keep the throttle wide open all the time, we still managed to achieve over 45mpg. Fitted with a two-gallon tank, the Suzuki has an enduro range of 90 miles, which in practical terms means that even in an event like the Welsh Two Day Trial, three fuel stops will be more than adequate. In trail riding terms, one tankful of petrol will give a really good day's riding, without having to hop from one village filling station to the next.

If your bike has poor fuel consumption, or the original tank capacity is inadequate, then some thought should be given to alleviating this problem. This will prove difficult with a bike like the Bultaco Frontera, which will gobble a gallon of fuel in 15 or 18 miles, but the minimum target to aim for should be fifty miles between fuel stops. When I rode works machines for Fantic, my bike was always the fiercest of the three team machines and consequently used most petrol. Even so, we managed to compromise so that the fuel consumption was never less than 30mpg, which meant that in enduros, we could refuel every 50 miles and still have some safety margin. The last bikes we had were quicker than the earlier ones and yet fuel consumption was dropping steadily until we were achieving 37mpg, which leads me to think that engines can still be made more economical, as well as being powerful.

The obvious immediate solution is to fit a bigger petrol tank and there are many excellent aluminium ones available to fit almost every bike ever produced. But bear in mind the earlier comments regarding carburation, for it is often possible to both increase power and reduce fuel consumption by fitting one of the very best modern carburettors.

In order to race on the rough, knobbly tyres are essential — and expensive. They also wear out far quicker than do trials tyres and require a certain skill when driving hard on the road. However, they are safe for road use and the bike can be made to go awfully quickly, without losing traction. The difficulty comes when they do break traction, because the resultant slide is usually quite violent, and comes without much warning. Therefore, if you choose to use knobbly tyres on tarmac, then do take care until you have acquired some experience as to how far they can be pressed.

Although to the neophyte one knobbly tyre looks much like another, there are important differences. An enduro tyre needs to be of a harder rubber compound and stiffer than a motocross tyre — although the two often overlap — and a few companies build extremely good tyres which take into account the specialist needs of the enduro rider. Metzeler, Continental and Barum all make excellent purpose-built tyres which wear well, and can be run at very low tyre pressures, without any detriment.

My present choice of tyres is the new Dunlop 'wet' MotoCross tyre at the rear — a formidable 5.00 x 18 inch chunk of rubber which gives incredible traction — and a 3.00 x 21 inch Metezler Motocross/Enduro at the front. This combination is remarkable in that the bike is stable under all conditions, including tarmac, and the tyres are also relatively hard wearing. The same choice is made by many Grand Prix motocross riders, so their pedigree is well founded, and the only drawback is that their purchase will knock a substantial hole in any rider's pocket.

When I rode for Fantic, the bikes were equipped with Metzeler ISDT tyres, and although difficult to find in England, these too, were very good. I remember in one disastrous event where I had managed to get three punctures and consequently had run out of spare inner tubes (and the spectators had long since gone home) I rode 15 miles with the inner tube of the rear tyre in shreds and yet the tyre itself suffered no harm. In fact, we used it on the spare bike for about another thousand miles and although the tread was very worn, the wall was still in perfect condition. Had a normal tyre been driven this distance flat, or even one of a scrambles pattern, the wall would have undoubtedly been destroyed. I mention this only to give some succour when the price of the special enduro tyre you have ordered is announced by the gloating parts assistant — it **is** worth the money.

From now on, the work is confined to fine tuning. On the Crooks Suzuki, all this work is done for the prospective owner, so that the bike is race-ready as it leaves the shop.

One of the most important modifications is the provision of a tool box, or bag, where the essential bits and pieces to make emergency repairs may be stored. Some riders prefer to carry their tools in a body belt or bag. I am very much against this system on two counts. Firstly, because I like to be free of as much weight as possible when I am riding, and secondly, and far more important, if the rider does fall and there is a pair of pliers between him and the ground, the consequences can be very painful.

On the Suzuki, I fitted a beautiful Italian leather tool bag, which a friend obtained for me in Italy for a very reasonable cost. Two ½ inch x 1/8 inch mild steel strips were welded to the rear frame loop, and the bag attached to these. The finished job looks like a production item from Suzuki.

One point of interest regarding the fitting of the bag, which has a universal lesson — never make a bracket

The new 'wet' Dunlop 5.00'' x 18'' is ideal for enduros

A leather tool bag adds the finishing touches to the bike

too strong. There are two reasons for this. Firstly, the stronger the fabrication is, the heavier it will be — as a general rule. Also, if something is weak enough to bend, and then be forced back into place, this is a far better state of affairs than making a super strong structure which will break on impact, probably damaging the bike's frame in the process.

My riding style dictates a low gear-lever, placed right on top of my foot. This is particularly bad on the Suzuki since the gear-lever already juts out more than the ideal, and is therefore especially prone to hitting obstructions, although not nearly so susceptible as many knowledgeable riders (including myself) originally imagined. Knowing that it is likely to get hit, I have drilled its length so that should a collision occur, the lever bends easily rather than breaking or worse still, damaging the gear selector shaft.

The suspension on the Suzuki is already very good and with no attention whatsoever will be adequate for an average rider in an enduro. However, it can be improved, and I have found that an SAE 30 hydraulic oil, combined with checking that both front fork springs are the same length, improves matters tremendously. The rear dampers are not the ultimate in sophistication but unlike most Japanese units, they are quite satisfactory.

Most modern trail bikes have front forks with internal springs and exposed stanchions. This style of suspension used to be called Ceriani in honour of the Italian firm who pioneered the design and on early forks, the seals were not sufficiently good to permit adequate wiping of each stanchion before the slider passed over it. Even today, riders will say "Ceriani forks leak oil", when what they really mean is that synthetic seals in 1965 were less than perfect.

By the mid 1970s, the problem was solved by the introduction of fat, spongy fork seals and now, front fork seals can be expected to last a long time, even in the most severe conditions. However the stanchions are still vulnerable, if neglected. Ironically, their greatest enemy is not the mud and rocks of the hardest trail run but the salt put on winter roads. In fact, a bike used for hard riding often fares better regarding fork life than does one which never strays from the tarmac, since the latter does not use all its front fork movement and consequently the stanchion does get wiped clean. The sensible rider will physically clean the stanchion of his bike every time it has been exposed to salt or any other nasty substance which might pit the surface of the hard chrome. A wipe with an oily rag will ensure that it stays in perfect condition.

The obvious solution is to totally enclose the rear chain as Jawa and Bultaco both do on their machines. An ISDT Jawa will cover 1,500 miles in the worst conditions imaginable, with only one chain adjustment. By comparison, my Suzuki, producing less power and ridden rather more slowly, needs attention after only 150 miles, merely because the chain is exposed to the elements.

This chain guard helps reduce, though not prevent, chain wear. Back sheet is polythene and top-run is 'U' channel aluminium

It is difficult, bordering on impossible, to make a fully enclosed rear chain system on the Suzuki without having a quickly detachable rear wheel and a new gearbox cover casting. Within the brief which Eddie Crooks laid down, there was obviously no scope for the exercise, which is complicated and expensive and few riders will want to do it unless they were very serious about racing. Since the Suzuki is a fair example of modern trail bikes, we may fairly say that this situation exists for the majority. This being the case, we are faced with a series of alternatives which are very much second best.

First, choose a good chain in the largest size available. I use the massive 5/8 inch x 3/8 inch Renolds Super chain, so called because it was designed to deal with the power of the latest large capacity superbikes. This is good chain, but like its competitors, frighteningly expensive. It will be worn out after a thousand miles and the thought appals me when I think that the same chain on Renolds test bench can handle three times the Suzuki's power for 100,000 miles, merely by enclosing it and providing constant lubrication, in an oil bath.

Lubrication is most important and I use Duckhams Chain Lube during an enduro and clean and boil the chain in Duckhams Chainguard, a thick, lanolin-based grease, afterwards, if conditions have been really severe. I mention Duckhams by name not because I ride for the company, although I have enjoyed support from them in the past, but rather because in the field of chain lubrication, there is no other product available at the moment which compares with their's. In fact, an aerosol chain lube is marketed under the joint Renolds-Duckhams banner, which, knowing how chary Renolds are of being associated with any other company's product, speaks volumes for the qualities of Chain Lube. The precise uses of both products are discussed more fully when we come to examine machine maintenance in Chapter 9.

A chainguard is useful for deflecting tyre-wash — the water thrown up by the rear wheel — which is probably the biggest cause of chain wear. I fabricated a more effective one for the Suzuki since, like all Japanese bikes, the standard item is just a skimpy joke.

For the main part of the guard, I used a sheet of high-density polythene, since this has the advantage of being almost impervious to damage when, as often happens, it fouls a rock or a large tree stump. Aluminium is easier to work with but bends and fractures rather too easily for use on a racing bike, although quite adequate for normal trail use.

The Suzuki's gearbox sprocket is well enclosed and the cover needs to be cut back to prevent mud-packing in this area. Most modern trail bikes suffer from this problem so it will have to be rectified on almost any conversion job. Unfortunately, since the prosecution of a trials rider for riding with the gearbox sprocket exposed — a most petty and pedantic affair — the A-CU will not allow bikes to start in enduros without a cover on the

Gearbox sprocket cover is cut away to reduce the tendency of mud to pack behind it

gearbox sprocket. Since there is a legal precedent established, prosecution would be automatic if an over-zealous police officer decided to make a case of a bike ridden without the necessary covering.

Many trail riders use a chain tensioner so that they can have a whole day's riding without the need to adjust the chain. These tensioners are curved blocks of very hard rubber which are brought to bear on the underside of the chain by spring tension. As the chain wears, the tensioner rises and takes up the slack. They also work well in reverse by absorbing the lash from the chain when the engine is over-run, so giving a much smoother ride.

If I used the Suzuki exclusively for trail riding then I would fit one of these simple devices, but for enduros they have two drawbacks. First, they absorb power, since the chain has to slide over a stationary object. An engineering friend who researches into frictional losses estimates that the power loss could be as much as 10% when the chain is dry, and by dry, the inference is free of lubrication rather than lacking in water. It takes a lot of time in the workshop to gain a 10% increase, without having it lost for no good purpose.

Secondly, they are another aspect of the bike which may go wrong. Hanging beneath the chain, the potential for snagging on rocks or getting caught in tree roots is sufficiently great to dissuade me from fitting one.

Used under the hardest conditions, I would estimate that the Suzuki's fork seals will have a life of about 5,000 miles. After renewal, they should last a further 5,000 miles before the whole fork is worn out. After 10,000 miles of racing use, I think that the rest of the bike will be so battered that the forks will be the least of your problems. This being the case, the question of the rubber fork gaiters which some riders use in an attempt to prolong fork life, becomes an academic one. Fork gaiters do not keep ALL the dust out of the stanchions and they tend to retain in a confined area the debris which does penetrate. They also effectively discourage the rider from the sort of continuous maintenance which we just discussed, since only the most zealous mechanic will go to the trouble of removing the fork gaiters after every ride, in order to clean the sliders. That two minute wipe over with an oily rag becomes an hour and a half's chore.

The situation is markedly different if the bike is used in motocross, because in this sport, earth and rocks will be hurled at the bike in such quantity that it is often impossible for the sliders to remove it. Also a number of marques with long-travel front suspension have begun adopting the external fork springs, so that the vast length of spring does not retain too much of the damping oil, as would happen if there were an internal spring. So if you decide to make your trail bike look like a real racer, then it is as well to realise the implications of authenticity.

On an older machine, with external fork springs fitted as standard, fork gaiters are essential, since these forks were never designed to be operated in dust and mud. Anything which can be done to protect them, should be. I had a vintage Triumph Cub trials bike which I used in four-stroke trials, and this had big, heavy front forks which leak oil everywhere, as well as having a markedly inferior action to modern units.

Bushes wore out at a frightening rate and whilst salt was no threat, since everything was continually coated in oil, the conditions found at even the most gentle trial did them no good at all. Obviously the layer of rubber which kept out the big lumps of dirt was very useful, but by the same token, there is no way I was going to get 5,000 miles of trials use from one set of front fork bushes. One major enduro would probably wreck them.

I cannot conceive of any situation where fork gaiters, fitted to a modern machine would help, and the only major company I know which does adopt this approach is Jawa. And if I had to fit Czech oil seals to my bike, I think I too, would fit gaiters.

Many of the less exotic trail bikes suffer from very poor rear damping and often the handling can be much improved by substituting the original dampers for a pair of Girling gas shocks or Konis. Again, it is a case of consulting the experts, before spending any money. If you are a relatively inexperienced rider, it might also be useful to seek the assistance of a motocross rider or an experienced enduro competitor, who can help set up your bike by riding at considerably faster speeds than you can manage, since handling characteristics vary greatly depending on the speed at which the bike is being driven.

Chain wear is always a problem on any trail bike and difficulty is especially great on a competition machine. A chain is really a series of roller bearings, just like those used to support the crankshaft in the engine. Imagine pouring sand and water through crankcases so that the main bearings and big-ends were permanently immersed in abrasive. Horrific though it sounds, this is just what we do to a chain when we go trail riding in wet conditions.

On balance, I think that fitting a chain tensioner would be a good modification for all normal trail riding, but for those 10% of riders whose riding is confined to really tough going, or racing, then the drawbacks outweigh the advantages.

In this trim, our TS 250 has proved to be very competitive as an enduro machine, particularly in view of its

The Suzuki in its final stages — a competition thoroughbred with looks to match

The transformation is complete and the once docile and domesticated Japanese trail bike is now a real racer. In this trim it won medals in both the ultra-tough ISCA 150 and the 1976 Welsh Two Day Trial

relatively low cost. It goes well, stops well, handles beautifully (once its little idiosyncrasies are mastered) and is reliable.

It is not perfect by a long way. A little more power, a six-speed gearbox, a better air-filtration system and a fully enclosed rear chain would improve the bike considerably. Even so, it has proved to be a very competitive mount being fast enough to win medals in both the ISCA 150 and the Welsh Two Day and setting special test times which compare favourably with genuine racing bikes. It will also tackle any green lane track that I can conceive and is sufficiently docile for more sedate trail riding, on the rare occasions I ask it to perform this task.

If any bike has the same basic virtues as the Suzuki, then it, too, can be made to perform in the same way. Not only will the rider's pleasure be much increased on the trail, but the actual modifications are also great fun. But please remember to think first, then ask the experts, then check and finally bend, saw or buy. It's the only way to happy tuning.

6 Riding equipment

Let me begin this Chapter by saying that there is no set of clothing perfectly suitable for trail riding. Everything I have tried has some major weakness and the best that can be achieved is to choose the most effective from the available products, and suffer their inadequacies quietly.

If we consider the demands which trail riding makes on clothing, the reason why so many manufacturers have failed so consistently becomes readily apparent.

Paramount for normal trail riding must be a high degree of weather protection. The riding suit must be waterproof, even in the kind of rain which is only found on a hill-track in winter. Secondly, the garment must be tough and resistant to tearing on branches and rocks, and abrading by extended contact with water and mud. The suit will be of little value if it is not supple and light, so that full body movement is both possible and comfortable. Finally, it should not be so hot that riding is made uncomfortable in more clement weather and preferably it should breathe, like leather, so that excessive perspiration does not become a problem. The same criteria may be applied to footwear, although there are some further demands in this specialised field, which we will discuss later.

What we appear to be seeking is a jacket and trouser suit made from thin leather — were it not for the fact that even the best leather is not waterproof. A pvc suit would be ideal from the weather aspect except that it would be hopelessly hot in warm weather on a hard ride, and stiff and uncomfortable when cold. Nylon suits are better, being light and reasonably waterproof, but one brush with a hawthorn bush and the material will be shredded. Such suits do have their place in trail riding, but it is not normally to be employed in general and regular use.

So the choices spiral gradually but inevitably down to two basic garments made by three manufacturers. These are the waxed cotton suits made by the Belstaff and Barbour companies and the polyurethane and cotton garments made by TT Leathers, who also produce a waxed cotton suit.

Without wishing to offend either manufacturer, I think that it is fair to say that the Barbour and Belstaff suits are basically the same, so the comments which I am going to make about the Belstaff may be applied to both

Belstaff begin by choosing a long staple yarn Egyptian cotton, which is closely woven to form the basis for their suit. This material is strong and resistant to tearing. Even better, when a hole is abraded in it, the frayed material tends not to run, and the hole will rarely get any bigger. The fabric is then treated with a special wax, the formulation of which is a closely guarded trade secret. Finally, a detachable cotton lining is added, which gives a good degree of warmth.

The initial line of defence against the ingress of water is the wax, because it has been forced into every pore of the fabric, and therefore acts as an effective water-repellant. When the water eventually does overcome the wax barrier, the cotton fibres swell, and the pores of the fabric close up, just as a tent does when wet.

However, because there are holes (in fact, microscopic gaps which number millions to the square inch) in the fabric, it can breathe, and perspiration can be kept down to a tolerable level. Here then, we have a suit which is waterproof, strong and wears well. Unfortunately, it does have one main disadvantage — an ability to attract dirt.

It does not ask too much creativity to imagine what is going to happen to a sticky surface, when it is exposed to mud and dust. If, like me, you have no particular desire to finish every expedition with dirty, sticky hands, then you will not find the thought of a waxed cotton suit an attractive one. But the fact of the matter is

Equipped like this, a rider can cope with any conditions in comparative comfort. The suit is waxed cotton and strong enduro boots are worn. Note also the A-CU approved helmet, large MX peak and Carrera goggles. MX gloves are also worn for maximum comfort

that in my experience, only this suit will keep you dry whilst meeting the other demands of trail riding. Ironically, the cleaner the suit becomes through wear, the less water-repellant it is likely to become. It would seem to be a classic case of swings and roundabouts.

After much hard use, the waxed cotton suit can be re-proofed (thus restoring its waterproof qualities) at home, although this is an extremely messy job. Belstaff sell re-proofing kits with full instructions, and would probably do the job for you if they were bombarded with pleading letters, even though re-proofing is not work they normally undertake.

The Belstaff concern is one member of quite a large group of companies with extensive research facilities and they are continually experimenting with new materials and processes. Even so, in the opinion of their managing director, Mr. W. Fieldhouse, there will be nothing to replace the waxed cotton material in the foreseeable future. This is an interesting statement and one which casts doubt on the second suit which we are going to discuss, the polyurethane-coated cotton type.

One answer to the serious trail rider's clothing problems are these enduro jeans which came on to the market just as this book was published. They are made from waxed cotton, strengthened with leather and have plastic kneecaps for maximum protection

This material, known widely in the trade as Armathene or Vystram, was pioneered by the TT Leathers concern, at Barnard Castle in Tyne and Wear. The process is beautifully simple and has many attractions from the trail rider's point of view. A cotton cloth, similar to that used by Belstaff, is coated with polyurethane on one face. Polyurethane is a type of plastic which is waterproof, flexible, very tough and has the property of osmosis, ie. the transfer of water-vapour (perspiration) through tiny pores. The material's water resistance is not as good as that of the waxed cotton suit but the cloth is perfectly clean to the touch.

There is one big drawback. Wherever there is a seam in the suit, great difficulty is experienced in sealing this area against the ingress of water and similarly, every stitch hole (and there are thousands in each suit) is a potential entrance for water. When these holes are not sealed by the waxed suit's combination of swelling fibres and wax, they invariably let in water. The only solution is periodically to treat every seam with water-proofing wax, which is available from TT, but this procedure puts us back to square one regarding the dirt. Most riders accept that they are going to get wet in heavy rain, if they wear one of these suits.

The author in action in the 1975 Welsh Two Day Trial, wearing a polyurethane suit and getting thoroughly wet in the process! These suits are very comfortable, particularly for racing, but do not have the water-repellant qualities of waxed cotton

That many riders do choose these suits is due to their other properties. The TT garments are exceptionally well cut for the competition rider, particularly in the trousers, which are a tight fit and are heavily reinforced with leather on the inside of the knee. This is very useful since it not only protects the trousers from excessive wear but also provides some sort of a barrier between the rider's leg and terra firma when he hits the ground.

A major criticism of the TT suits is that they are totally unlined and being a tight fit, it is not easy to wear sufficient underneath the suit to make winter riding comfortable. This is never a problem to the competition rider or even the man who is going for a day's hard trail riding — the sport is sufficiently strenuous to make sure you are never cold. The difficulty sets in when wearing the suit for extended periods — that is, anything over an hour — of road riding. TT are going to offer a detachable lining as an optional extra in the near future and this should cure this problem.

The final area of differences between the two types of suit is largely cosmetic and how much importance, if any, you attach to it is very largely subjective. The waxed cotton suits are never very bright, even when new. The colours are limited to black, red and green and when the dyed cloth has been coated with wax these are invariably very subdued hues. In contrast, there is no limit at all to the colour range of polyurethane suits. My present outfit is black and flurescent orange and prior to this, I enjoyed a fetching shade of pillar box red. After much wear, the colours are still strong, unlike the waxed cotton suits which tend to blend with the mud to form a green/brown, red/brown, or black/brown mixture — ideal for guerilla warfare. Personally, I rather like my black and orange outfit and the thought of returning to a waxed cotton dullness does not excite me. However, other riders cherish the badge of honour which a soiled Belstaff represents and would probably choke if they were made to wear a brightly coloured outfit. The choice must be a subjective one.

One of the reasons that the polyurethane suit does look better is that it can be regularly washed. My team manager, pit crew and chief mechanic (she is also my wife) hand-washes the suit in warm, soapy water and then rinses it. And it comes out like a Tide advert. You MUST NOT wash a waxed cotton suit under any circumstances since this will remove the all-important wax from the fabric. When the Belstaff suit is dirty, it must be cleaned with clean, cold water, just as you would do the bike, and left to dry naturally. This means that next time you come to wear the suit, it will be stiff and grubby, an idea which does not appeal to me.

On balance, I would say that for non-competitive trail riding, where there is a need for complete weather protection and warmth on road rides, the waxed cotton suit is a better buy — providing of course, the sartorial element has no influence in your decision. For competition use, where the rider needs complete freedom of movement and is likely to get his riding gear very dirty, then I prefer the polyurethane coated suit.

Having said this, my feelings are not so strong either way that I could not be persuaded to change my mind by some cogent argument.

If you are wondering why I have restricted this discussion to just two types of suit produced by three manufacturers it is because in my experience, these are the only alternatives in a sport which taxes quality and design to the utmost.

Both the suits I have mentioned are of a two-piece design, have strong, long-wearing zips and sensible pockets — simply, they are the products of experienced companies who are familiar with the demands made by trail riding and have designed equipment to meet them. They in no way hold a monopoly on the market, except in the de facto sense that few firms will go to the expense and trouble of designing suitable clothing. Only a few months prior to writing these words, a company engaged in the manufacture of mountaineering clothing sent me a suit to try out. It was made from yet another wonder material and its designers assured me that it would stand up to any conceivable rigour. The first time I wore it in real Welsh rain I got soaked and within three weeks it was a tattered collection of rags. When I sent the thing back with some rather caustic comments, the management threw up their hands in disgust, "The suit", they expostulated, "was NOT designed for that sort of wear and tear!" Something at which I could only laugh.

The products made by Barbour, TT and Belstaff all have faults but they will stand up to the hardest treatment a dirt rider can hand out, week in and week out, and this is the most important thing. Possibly by the time I have written this there will be a new, miracle suit which will be clean, waterproof and as tough as oxhide. I hope so. However, I have seen more white elephants in the field of motorcycling clothing than in the rest of the motorcycle world together. View any new product with extreme suspicion and though callous as it may seem, let someone else have the pleasure of enjoying the miracle before you put your money on the counter. If there is a success story, it will soon get around.

An equally expensive, and important item of clothing, is your foot covering. Again the choice is confined to two main areas — boots, or industrial wellingtons.

A pair of purpose-designed leather enduro boots will be superbly comfortable, even for ten hours a day. They will also leak water, cost a lot of money and might well save a broken leg or sprained ankle if you ever decide to go racing. A pair of reject 'trials wellies', as the industrial wellingtons are known colloquially, will cost a quarter the amount and will never let in water, and might end your riding career if they get caught on a tree root or rock at speed.

Again the choice largely depends whether it is proposed to include racing in the rider's trail riding activities. If it is, then quite categorically leather boots should be choosen from both the comfort and safety angles. The type of boot which is suitable for enduros, and therefore for trail riding, will be one very similar to that used in motocross. That is, a strapped boot with good protection for the instep, shin and ankle. The sole should be of a slipper design — one piece sole and heel without a sharply defined heel — but unlike motocross boots, where the sole is often perfectly smooth, there should be some ribs or cleating, to provide grip when the bike has to be pushed.

If the sole does have a block heel then there is a very good chance that this will catch behind some obstacle as the rider uses his foot for balance. Having had this happen at high speed — I was trying a new motocross machine at the time and had slipped on a pair of trials wellingtons which were to hand — I can vouch from personal experience that it is very painful.

There are some very good boots on sale at present made by specialist manufacturers such as Sidi, Ashmans, Daytona and a Czech brand imported into Britain by CZ, and these are made expressly for enduro riding and will give the sort of protection and wear that should be expected. My own favourite is the enduro version of the 74/06 from Ashmans, which has the same upper as the MX design but has a ribbed slipper sole instead of a completely smooth one. This provides just sufficient grip to provide some purchase on wet rocks or mud but not so much that it prevents the foot from floating over obstacles at speed.

Although there is some disagreement on this point. I feel that only a boot derived from a motorcross design will be effective for trail riding. Trials boots, which are rather like wellingtons in design, just do not give a sufficiently firm fitting to be comfortable at racing speeds and the sole design is usually inadequate.

All leather boots will leak water after prolonged exposure but a good boot will keep you warm, safe and dry, even after a hard day's trail riding. I wear a thin pair of normal socks and a thick, woollen pair of sea-socks with my Ashman's boots (the thicker pair being needed for added protection) and at the end of a hard winter enduro, my feet will still be more or less dry although the outer socks will be damp. This is adequate for me and if you need perfect waterproofing, then wellingtons are the answer.

Before discussing the alternative, a word of warning should be sounded against trying to waterproof boots by over-zealous application of dubbin. All the boots I have quoted are made from fine, high quality leather, which is both stiff and strong. Too much dubbin can make this leather soft and flexible, thus destroying its protective qualities. It is better to apply the dubbin only when the leather is very dry and use ordinary shoe polish, liberally applied, on other occasions. Never, ever try to dry leather boots artificially by a fire, since this can cause the leather to burn internally and will definitely make it stiff and brittle. If you are really desperate, a hair dryer will help do the job safely but this takes some hours and is naturally an expensive process.

Industrial wellingtons require none of the love and attention which boots demand. When they are dirty, inside or out, a good scrub and hose down will bring them up to pristine condition — and this can be repeated indefinitely. Trials wellies are ideal for the rider who wishes to ride gently along the trails and who has a rather limited budget. They have all the disadvantages of having the wrong sort of sole for speed work and also being a rather slack fit on the ankle, but used sensibly, they will provide excellent service for minimal cost. Certainly, they have proved a blessing to observed trials riders, where about 90% of competitors wear them.

Note that the wellingtons must be of the industrial type and not the normal, wander-about-the-garden boots. These wellingtons, usually made by Dunlop, have a steel toe cap, strongly raised ribs on the inside of the ankle and down the front of the boot and one or two steel plates underneath the instep. They also have a very thick sole and are generally of a rugged construction. Originally, they were designed for construction workers and heavy industrial work and therefore are well able to cope with the rigours of trail riding.

Do not, under any circumstances, ride in anything other than good, strong purpose-designed footwear, since this will guarantee a short, miserable and painful trail riding career. It is also a good way to see if there are any nurses worth chatting up at your local orthopaedic department.

Apart from the legal necessity to wear a helmet whenever you ride on a public highway, a law which I imagine is valid for green lanes as well as those which are tarmaced, common sense dictates that one's head should always be protected. There is a greater chance of falling from your machine while trail riding than there is

The new Ashmans enduro boot compared with the Dunlop trials wellington. The enduro boot has a slipper sole and gives much more protection. It also costs five times as much as an industrial wellington

Alpine Star make these purpose built enduro boots. They are extremely strong and have been developed from the firm's MX boots with the addition of a cleated sole that some grip is afforded when rescuing the bike from bogs

on the road since both you and the bike will be tested to a greater degree than is normal. This is what makes trail riding fun and it is also the reason why the very best in head protection should always be worn. Never be swayed by the argument that because you are riding slowly, there is little danger involved. If you go over the handlebars at five miles an hour and land on a rock or tree root, then it will hurt. Should your head be unprotected, then the consequences could be unpleasant. Trail riding has an impressive safety record and every attempt should be made by the neophyte to maintain this. In discussing helmets, we shall look at only those suitable for enduros — that is, A-CU approved for racing. A helmet which meets these standards will be perfectly satisfactory for any other trials use, whilst a lower standard one, whilst legal for the road, is nothing but a dangerous liability.

In choosing a helmet, the rider should be aware of two things. First of all, does it meet a sufficiently high standard to give adequate protection for the sport and secondly, is it comfortable so that it can be worn happily for hours on end during a trail ride?

The key approval tags to look for are British Standard 1869 and the American Standard Z90.1 ANSI. British Standard 1869 is the standard set as the MINIMUM acceptable for helmets to be used in Britain for racing and although somewhat outdated (it is at the moment under review) it is nevertheless an indication of adequacy. The American Standard Z90.1 tests the helmet's ability to withstand high impact and they are considered to be most worthwhile by helmet manufacturers, although unlike the BSI tests, the Z90.1 series is conducted on one batch of helmets and not on a continuous random sampling of production examples.

Other labels might tell you that the helmet is approved for racing by the A-CU (in Britain) or the AMA (in America) but apart from needing the stamp of these organisations to be considered eligible for their events, they can be disregarded, since neither body knows enough about helmets to make any judgement as to their suitability or otherwise for racing.

Another common standard amongst the better helmets is the Snell Institute's 1970 standard, which at the moment seems to be given only to glass-fibre helmets, regardless of the performance of other types. I do not know enough about the reasons, either technical or political, for the Snell Institute's reluctance to accept other materials, but I do know that there are some very fine helmets made in polycarbonate — the only viable alternative to glass fibre for racing helmets — and it would be a pity to disregard these totally.

At the present time, helmets are constructed largely from glass-fibre, polycarbonate, or ABS. Glass-fibre is probably the superior material, since it is light, strong, absorbs and dissipates shock very well and reacts favourably to paint, solvent, hair oil and hydrocarbons such as petrol or oil. It is also the most expensive material to work with, since it requires a number of labour intensive activities to manufacture the helmet. Glass-fibre helmets also give an attractive finish.

Various BSI helmet standards

Griffin helmet, with essential peak for competition riding. The peak in this helmet is the sophisticated Torsten Hallman model whose angle can be altered whilst riding

A close second is polycarbonate, which is a good material except for the way it dissipates shock — by revolving a chain of molecules within the helmet's structure instead of physically disintegrating, as would a glass-fibre shell. This, in my opinion, is not as successful as the sacrificial destruction of the shell. Polycarbonate is also affected by the solvents in most paint so it is absolutely forbidden to paint a helmet made from this material.

Helmets made from polycarbonate are manufactured by the injection moulding process, in which the powdered polymer is first melted and then squeezed into a mould. Except for the very high cost of the mould, this is a cheap method of manufacture and consequently your helmet can be sold at a much lower price than a fibre-glass item.

ABS is of no use whatsoever and is simply unsuitable for our purposes. The material is susceptible to ultra-violet degradation and although it is possible to purchase helmets carrying BS 1869 in ABS, it should be remembered that their efficiency decreases markedly with age. Like polycarbonate, what protection they offer will be reduced if they are painted. ABS is also adversely affected by a number of solvents commonly found in or around the paddock.

For those non-technical riders, ultra-violet comes mainly from the sun's radiations so your ABS helmet is decomposing before your very eyes every time you ride. After six months, an ABS helmet begins to deteriorate rapidly and the rider trusts to his luck from then on. He might be fortunate and get away unscathed but then he might not. And like any sport, there is sufficient element of risk in trail riding not to invite trouble.

Comfort is of prime importance to any rider, and when purchasing a helmet it should be remembered that one's head swells during the course of an enduro — with exertion mainly, but a modicum of success helps as well — and so the helmet should be a firm, but not tight fit.

In my many years of competition I have purchased and worn many different helmets from many different manufacturers: Everoak, Premier, Bell and AGV to name but a few. Each, at the time, had something special to offer — although during the late 60s when clothing manufacturers blossomed to cater for the tremendous boom in motorcycle sport, one was influenced by fashion and other unimportant design features towards a particular helmet. Only in the fullness of time does one learn what is and what is not important to one's own requirement. If I can pass on a little of my own experience — all paid for in pound notes and tales of woe — I would suggest the following criteria:

Safety: Is the helmet well-made? Is it approved for racing and does it afford the wearer a good margin of protection? Does it cover the temples and forehead? Is it cut away at the nape of the neck? Does it have a strong, but easily unfastened buckle?

Comfort: Does it have provision for a peak to be firmly attached? Is it a firm, but not too tight fit? If it can be waggled around when fastened to the head, imagine what it will do at speed over rough terrain. Is it too heavy for real comfort? Do the fastening straps chafe under the chin?

Price: The old adage, "If you have a ten bob head, get a ten bob helmet", does not hold much water these days. Although price is a fair indication of quality, bear in mind that imported helmets will carry an inflated price tag due to duties and taxes and will therefore upset the comparison between imported and home produced items of the same quality. Glass-fibre is the best of modern materials and prices will run considerably higher than those for other materials. However, polycarbonate is a good second and becoming progressively better. Look for the approval tags on each helmet and short-list them, try each one of your choice and make up your mind. To help you, just take note of what the top line professionals are wearing, for although it is true to say that they are being paid for wearing one particular manufacturer's product, very few I know would wear sub-standard helmets at any price.

Before leaving the subject of helmets, a comment should be made about their working life. Most helmets have an impact absorbing liner which loses its effectiveness after a severe crash. Similarly, modern helmet shells are designed for one really heavy crash, and no more. Not, I would hasten to add, because manufacturers are too parsimonious to build stronger shells, but because it was discovered that an unbreakable shell transmits shock so well that it can damage a rider's brain just as much as if he were to hit the track wearing no head protection at all.

Finally, the general wear and tear and abrasive forces of competition ensure that a helmet becomes markedly less effective after a couple of seasons and it is advisable to replace it, even though no visible damage may be apparent.

Whilst a two piece suit, boots and a good helmet will provide all the protection and comfort any trail rider could desire, even on the most arduous outing, if regular competitive riding is going to be undertaken, then some alternatives must be considered.

Although enduros are nominally reliability events, the trend is increasingly towards making them long-distance motocross races. This means riding flat out most of the time and slightly faster than flat out for the rest. Obviously, there is going to be little spare time to correct unsuitable and uncomfortable riding gear and equally, the chances of your falling — and even the very best riders do — are going to be increased the harder one rides.

So, the first thing to ensure before riding in an enduro is that your riding gear is comfortable — and will stay comfortable for eight hours.

Many riders use their riding suits for enduros and find that they give them adequate protection. Certainly, in the winter events such as the Beacons or ISCA 150, a riding suit is the answer, because the courses are simply too wet for anything else to be a practical proposition. Also, because conditions are so difficult, speeds tend to be reduced, making things in general somewhat slower.

In dry events, the answer is to wear motocross leathers. These are strong, leather jeans with padded knees and thighs and provide tremendous protection. A good pair of motocross jeans will be proof against a river crossing or prolonged shower, but not for an extended period of rain, so one needs to be reasonably sure of fine weather before the start of the event. It is possible to wear leathers under a suit but this is not really a practical proposition. Two lots of covering on the legs are too much of a hindrance and riding becomes uncomfortable.

A further drawback is that the leathers chafe on the riding suit and wear out quickly and with the current price of leather garments, this is not to be recommended.

Racing in enduros is hard work, about that there can be no argument. Therefore any help which can be given to the body is sensible. Most motocross riders wear a body belt to help support their stomach and back muscles and this item of clothing is essential for enduros. A body belt is a strong, wide belt, made from leather, canvas or plastic, which when fastened should be firm but completely comfortable.

In dry weather, particularly if riding in enduros, MX jeans are ideal. Unfortunately they are also expensive but well made ones, like these Kershaw leathers, are worth the investment for the serious rider

I have an elasticated one, lined with very soft chamois leather, and this type is perhaps better than those which rely on buckles and straps for tension since it stays in adjustment indefinitely and is unaffected by perspiration.

Gloves are also very important — although one would not guess this seeing some of the tattered remnants worn by some riders — since a good pair of gloves will not only help prevent blistering but will give some protection against stones thrown up by the bike in front. Once again, motocross provides the answer and a visit to a specialist dealer will reveal a wide range to choose from. All these gloves will be purpose designed for racing and should have seamless palms and some form of protection for the back of the hand and fingers. Probably the best type of glove in the world is the Jofa anti-blister and although extremely expensive, it is standard equipment for 90% of grand prix riders. In my experience, there is nothing to touch it for comfort, quality and length of service, so perhaps the initial purchase price is vindicated.

One personal tip which I might offer in the field of gloves is a product which is sold by Boots — a liberally sized range of household gloves. I suffer terribly from cold hands and I simply could not ride with wet hands for an extended period, no matter how much I wanted to. This posed a problem, since the conventional over-mitts are far too clumsy for racing. The answer was the heavy duty rubber gloves which an Australian company makes, and Boots sell. I have a fairly big hand but even so, the extra large size in the range fitted over my Jofa gloves perfectly, keeping them dry and yet still maintaining full sensitivity for brake and throttle control.

Still the best gloves in the world for off road use, despite their cost, these Jofa MX gloves have padded palms to prevent blistering and reinforced fingers to deflect stones

When not in use, they will fold up easily into one of the large pockets which the riding suits we have discussed have in abundance and so are no hardship to carry in an event, even if not used.

Finally, we come to eye protection — perhaps the most important item of all. Most riders have a motocross peak attached to their helmet, since this would provide a surprising amount of protection from stones thrown up by the bike in front. This is its primary purpose in motocross but in enduros it can be an invaluable buffer against rain blown horizontally by a gale force wind.

I would like to be able to say never remove goggles when racing, but it is often simply impractical — perhaps impossible is even more accurate — to ride with goggles down. In the 1975 Welsh Two Day, it rained so hard on the first day that my Carrera goggles, which have a substantial slit in the bottom of the lens, were actually filled up with rain. Much as I dreaded doing it, the only solution was to remove them. In this case, the peak is worth its weight in gold as a buffer between the rider's exposed eyes and rain which seems to be made from steel rods.

The choice of goggles is largely a personal thing. However, once again they must be completely comfortable for long periods and they must also have plastic lenses which will not shatter if struck by a stone. My choice — and one which is supported by many leading enduro riders and motocrossers — is the Austrian Carrera goggle, a light ski goggle with a very wide field of vision. Another good choice are the scooter eye shields, rather like a pair of spectacles with a large, one piece lens. These are particularly good in very wet conditions but are not so good as the Carrera in dust.

It is worth remembering that compared with trail riding, your first enduro will seem like hard labour in Siberia. With this in mind, try not to wear too many clothes under your riding suit, even in winter. I wear a pair of swimming trunks, since support is vitally necessary when motoring fast, some thin corduroy jeans and my suit's trousers. On top, a motocross shirt, which will soak up the sweat, and a thin pullover under my jacket, is all that I need, even in a blizzard. Some riders wear even less than this.

For a summer enduro, I would discard the pullover and probably wear motocross leathers instead of the over-trousers — certainly no more, since freedom of movement is essential. Faced with a really hot event, I think the best solution would be to ride in leathers and a shirt, as do many of the Continental riders. And I only hope you have the chance to ride this way in Britain on some occasion — I'm still waiting!

7 Basic riding technique

Riding on the rough is not like road riding! The novice would do well to learn that statement by heart and repeat it every time he goes trail riding. The biggest difference lies in the amount of grip the riding surface offers. Using modern tyres on a tarmaced road surface — even a wet one — it is virtually impossible to get into a skid, if the machine is driven in a sensible manner. On trails, it is almost impossible to get any grip on some surfaces, even with an expert on the throttle.

Every surface on a trail offers different grip and in six months you will be able to recognise and evaluate every one of them, on sight. Roughly, they might be graded thus:

1   Moss-covered stone — extremely bad. Treat with great caution.
2   Clay type mud — very bad, but quite rideable.
3   Loose stones — bad, but satisfactory if treated gently.
4   Wet grass, particularly on a stone or clay base — tricky. Can be ridden fast but has the potential to lose all grip very suddenly.
5   Loose stones with liquid mud. No great problem except when travelling very fast.
6   Dry, dusty surfaces — can be treated like wet grass only more so. Will give excellent grip until the surface crumbles, so take care!
7   Damp marl, soft clay or wet sand — fantastic! Better grip than tarmac and virtually no limit to the speed at which the bike can be driven.

All these surfaces can be ridden by a beginner, on a very basic machine, PROVIDING they are tackled with a little forethought and at a sensible (ie slow) speed. The great majority of the difficulties arise when an element of speed is needed and to ride quickly on the rough does require a certain amount of skill and experience.

Before discussing the actual riding techniques, let us look briefly at what causes the rear wheel of a motorcycle to lose traction, and also what can be done to encourage it to find drive.

The engine of the machine transmits power to the rear wheel via the gearbox. The more power the engine gives then the greater will be the rear wheel's desire to spin. The more power applied by the rider, the greater the rear wheel's tendency to spin. Therefore, for the best traction, the engine should be giving as little power as is commensurate with adequate forward momentum.

Drive is also affected by the number of power impulses transmitted to the rear wheel. At high speed, the number of impulses per yard will be small, even at peak revs., because a high gear will be used. At low speed, the number of impulses can be high because a low gear, necessitating high rpm in order to maintain any forward speed, will be used.

A four-stroke machine, which has one power impulse for every four revolutions of the engine, will be giving much better drive than a two-stroke, which has a power impulse every two cycles. This is because for three revolutions, the four-stroke has decreasing power applied to the rear wheel and this reduces the chances of it tearing free from the earth.

The four-stroke engine can teach us a valuable lesson. To increase grip, the amount of power transmitted to the rear wheel must be DECREASED. To see this technique exploited to its greatest extent, one only has to watch an observed trial. Here the riders will slow the engine revs. down to almost nothing and then, quite suddenly, a wheel which has been spinning will find grip and the bike will clear the section. A good trail bike should be able to pull at zero revs. like a trials bike, but even if it doesn't, the technique is still viable at almost any point in the rev. range.

Using as high a gear as possible for any given speed is the best way to reduce the number of power impulses to the rear wheel, since the engine will have to rev. slowly to maintain the chosen ground speed. If you have an engine which will pull a high gear, then use its abilities wherever possible.

By now it should be clear that the throttle hand of the trail rider is his most important control.

It is as well not to be too ambitious when learning rough riding. There is ample scope for tying oneself in knots on the simplest section of trail, without actually seeking trouble. In fact, a piece of waste land, or a copse (providing you have obtained the owner's permission) is a good way to learn the basic techniques, without having to follow a six or seven mile trail through to the bitter end.

Select first or second gear, the higher the gear the better, so long as the motor is happy, and drive the bike at about 5-6mph. Make sure that the speed is kept constant and use the throttle gently, both to increase and decrease speed.

When coming to any rough sections, such as small ruts, hummocks, or a rise, stand up on the footrests so that the bike is balanced and your legs act as shock absorbers. Before actually meeting the obstacle, open the throttle slightly so that the bike is pulling. Any motorcycle always performs better on the rough when it is under power. This is an inviolable rule.

It is worth practising riding up, round and over obstacles with the engine pulling because this one technique, the ability to direct the bike as it accelerates, is the one which is going to be the most important of all when the time comes to actually trail ride. Initially, it might be best to slow down before reaching the slow section, in order that the bike can be accelerated over it. There is no shame in this and no prizes for falling off if you do not. Trail riding is a non-competitive activity to be enjoyed at the rider's own pace and in his own way.

If the bike is modern, or competition-based, and the obstacle is a sharp climb, then there is a chance that the front wheel will leave the ground. This is because the climb, combined with the machine's natural tendency to pivot round its back wheel under power, will make the front wheel rise. This is not as frightening as it sounds and is very easy to correct. Either moving the body forward so that the chest is more or less over the handlebars, or closing the throttle just a shade, will bring the front wheel gently to earth. After a time, you probably will not even bother to bring the wheel down unless things become really serious, since it is quite easy to hover the front wheel just off the ground merely by moving body weight. Second to throttle control, body movement is the most important aspect of trail riding. I would stress that it is vital to stand up on the footrests for any major manoeuvre or hazard, particularly when learning to ride a bike on the rough. Expert enduro riders seem to do everything sitting down, and manage to navigate their machines merely with a subtle movement of the elbow or shoulders. This is fine when you are ready for the ISDT, but not such a good idea until you can average 24mph along any mountain track in Britain.

All trail bikes steer better with the front wheel light, so every encouragement should be given for this to happen — within reason of course. Thus, when riding downhill, the rider's body should be moved to the rear of the bike with his bottom over the rear mudguard.

No matter how steep the hill, or treacherous the surface, the rear wheel should never be locked, either by engine braking or by use of the back brake. The reason for this golden rule is simple. A locked wheel which is skidding is not as effective a brake as one which is nearly locked, so in addition to not having full control over the bike — the rear wheel will be snaking all over the place if it is not free to turn — the bike will also be accelerating.

Most riders will be aware that when the throttle is closed, their machines will stop very quickly. This is because of engine braking — the force exerted by the engine compression and frictional losses on a motor which is producing no motive power. On a four-stroke, where the exhaust valve opens only once in four cycles, the engine braking will be greater than in a two-stroke machine where the piston exposes the exhaust port every two cycles. In either case, the engine braking is the most useful form of slowing a trail bike.

Depending on the steepness of the hill, select either first or second gear — the lower the gear, the greater the engine braking — and standing up, with the body weight well to the rear of the machine, gently steer the bike down the hill. Try to keep it both straight and upright, and relax, letting the suspension do the work for you. Never try to force a trail bike, particularly one which is derived from a competition machine, into doing anything. Being thoroughbreds, they often object in the strongest possible terms.

If the surface is very slippery, or the slope ultra-steep, there might be so much engine braking that the rear

Clay type mud — one of the worst types of riding surfaces. Here, the author is trying to force his way to the virgin mud on the left, which offers much better grip

Loose stones, washed clean as in this stream bed, provide quite good grip and present no real problem

Here the author has deliberately accelerated hard, so that the rear wheel spins on the clay surface. Closing the throttle is all that is needed to regain drive

Throttle control is perfect in this shot with the rider just keeping sufficient power to the rear wheel for optimum climbing ability but neither too much to cause wheelspin or for the bike to loop. Judging conditions to a fine degree should be practised until it becomes intuitive

All trail bikes should be ridden in a standing position on the rough, particularly if the rider is inexperienced

When approaching an obstacle, lean back and open the throttle and the front wheel will rise gently over it. This is true on even the most docile trail bike such as this 125cc Honda. When the rear wheel is locked on descent, even the most skilful rider experiences difficulty

Here, ISDT Silver Medal winner, Eddie Crooks, is struggling. He has had to pull in the clutch in order to free the back wheel and is now braking hard with the front brake to slow down. The photograph does not reflect the steepness of the descent nor its treacherous surface, which few spectators could walk up or down

When riding downhill, the rider's weight should be well to the rear of the machine

wheel locks. This happens more often with a four-stroke machine, because there is much greater braking power available. In this case, the next higher gear must be selected, even if this means an increase in speed.

Given careful use of both front and rear brake, a slow approach speed and a low gear, any slope up to a gradient of one in one can be ridden by an inexperienced rider, even if the surface is treacherous. The key to success is not to panic and this means having full confidence in the bike.

In my book on motocross, I recommended riders to practise using the front brake so hard that they could lock the front wheel and then control the resulting skid for three or four yards. To be able to do this at will is an essential for motocross and it is no bad thing for the average trail rider to be able to do. If you are familiar with applying the front brake hard and correcting any difficulties when they arise, then there will be no fears if you overbrake downhill and the front wheel breaks away.

Begin by practising quite slowly — about 15mph and apply the front brake until the wheel locks, keeping the throttle open and just accelerating. At this point, the wheel will probably try to go violently to one side or the other. Try to hold it for as long as possible — one second is ample time at first — and when things begin to get out of hand, simply release the front brake and the bike will straighten up with no trouble at all. The longer you can keep the wheel straight before it begins to "grab", the better rider you are becoming.

Of the two ends of the bike, slides at the front are the most difficult to control and also most likely to end with the rider hitting the ground. The rear wheel sliding around is less likely to cause any trouble and can even be beneficial in advanced riding.

It is a good idea to practise braking sufficiently hard to lock the front wheel

When the rear wheel breaks traction, it is likely to slide to one side or the other. The remedy is simple and failsafe. Partially close the throttle to stop wheelspin and at the same time turn the handlebar in the same direction as the rear wheel has stepped out of line. For example, if the rear wheel is sliding to the left, turn the handlebar to the left and the slide will be corrected. The technique is called 'opposite lock' and is used to the ultimate by grass track and speedway riders when power-sliding their machines.

With practice, you will find that correcting mild slides becomes so easy that it ceases to be a conscious effort. Certainly, when competing in an enduro, the rider can quite literally expect to spend hours correcting one slide after another, as the rear wheel drifts around under power on poor surfaces.

Other than by braking too hard, the front wheel should not lose traction in normal trail riding, unless the surface is very slippery. Generally, the inexperienced rider should exercise caution if the front wheel should start to drift, since things can get out of hand very quickly. The best method to correct a front end slide is to shut the throttle, leave the brakes completely alone, and try to get the bike as vertical as possible, since it is usually excessive angles of lean which are the cause of the trouble. To get the bike upright, prod firmly with the foot on the side towards which the bike is leaning. This sounds very easy on paper and in fact a good rider can give a judicious prod at 55mph and sort out quite a serious slide. Ernie Page passed me in the Welsh Two Day on a flat out forestry section, where we were both doing well over 65mph. In doing so, he ricocheted off an earth bank — a mere nothing to a rider of Ernie Page's calibre — and sorted out the resultant tangle with a mammoth lunge of his left leg, carrying on without so much as a hair out of place. However, until you have perfected this technique, be careful where you put your foot down.

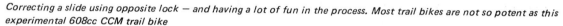

Correcting a slide using opposite lock — and having a lot of fun in the process. Most trail bikes are not so potent as this experimental 608cc CCM trail bike

The key is to place the foot in front of the bike with the toe raised. In doing this, you will be helped by the slipper sole of your boot, which should firstly give the bike some support and then be swept back and up on to the footrest as it is passed. Never point your toe downwards or place the foot flat on the ground so firmly that it cannot easily be flicked up. A 250lb motorcycle travelling at 30mph can do no end of nasty business to a foot which tries to get in its way. Similarly, never trail your leg behind the bike — no matter how cool you think it may look — since in doing this, there is a good chance that you will run over your own foot. If this does happen, try to do it in front of some spectators, since it is extremely funny to watch.

These then, are the basic techniques of trail riding — the tools with which to do the job. Now you must practise using them until they become second nature. Automatically, you should be standing up on the footrests, balancing the bike and ready to absorb shocks. If the rear wheel steps out of line, without thinking you will apply a touch of opposite lock and when the front wheel leaves the ground on a climb, your body will shift forward as if you had been riding on the rough from birth. Downhill you will be able to brake hard, confident in the knowledge that you can ride with the front wheel locked, if necessary, and your throttle hand will be as sensitive as a top-class surgeon's. Now you can tackle any trail in comfort, confident that you can enjoy the ride, no matter how hard it is.

This is my reason for urging practice before you go trail riding — and in my estimation, an undulating grass-covered lane which could be negotiated by the average family car is not trail riding. If you have confidence in yourself and equally important, confidence in the bike, then you can tackle the really challenging trails which makes the sport what it is. The lesser ones you will be able to manage without a second thought.

When sliding the bike, the foot used for support must be kept well up. The Triumph Adventurers, which made such a favourable impression a few years ago, were particularly pleasant to ride 'on the drift'

In the next Chapter, we will have a look at some of the techniques used to deal with a typical Welsh trail — the sort which would be used in one of the major enduros.

The author is risking getting his foot run over. Trailing a foot is bad practice and serves no purpose except to amuse onlookers when the bike runs over it

Lifting the front wheel is no problem at all with modern, competition orientated machines

8 Getting better all the time*

*With apologies to The Beatles

I would hope that sooner or later, well away from human habitation, walkers, horse riders or wandering entymologists, every trail rider will open up his bike and try to ride it quickly. I am a motocross rider and an ardent follower of this sport, but even so, blasting along a tough track that I have never seen before, has a very special attraction which not even motocross can equal. Similarly, watching a top-class enduro rider ease his way over incredibly tough terrain, without a flicker of effort, and at speeds which leave lesser mortals gasping in amazement, is a unique and gratifying experience.

Riding quickly on a trail is quite different from other forms of racing except, strangely, the TT road races in the Isle of Man. As in the Manx events, the racing is largely against the clock, with only an odd glimpse of the opposition to add spice to the proceedings. As such, the riding is a much more personal affair than motocross or grass track and the attraction is perhaps more intellectual than the gut appeal of track racing.

Enduros legitimize the normal desire for any rider with pride in his own ability to extend those skills used in riding by stretching his performance artificially. Faced with a tight schedule, one is forced to try harder and harder to achieve perfection in riding and speaking personally, this quest gives me great satisfaction. Some times I can get a fifty yard section of trail absolutely right and traverse it at near theoretical maximum speed. This is most satisfying, particularly if I can repeat the feat three or four times in an event. Then I am faced with the challenge of extending the 200 yards of perfection into 150 miles — which is what the top riders manage to do with monotonous regularity. It is certain that I will never approach perfection but there is a great sense of satisfaction in improving, little by little, the more I ride.

The last sentence is the key to why there are so many good enduro riders in their thirties and forties — an age when a motocrosser would have long since hung up his leathers. The secret is experience, for more than anything else, riding quickly on unseen tracks is a product of hard won experience. And for the same reason, it is possible to effect a continuous improvement for as long as the rider wishes to improve.

In this Chapter, we shall look at some of the simpler techniques of serious trail riding. Mastery of these, even assuming such competence could be gleaned from a book, will not guarantee a medal at the first event entered or a trouble free ride over a vicious Welsh trail in the middle of winter. Rather they will, hopefully, provide an awareness of some of the starting points for real riding. How far you want to go in the search for skill and perfection is entirely dependent on your interest.

One of the most useful techniques to acquire is that of lifting the front at will. With a modern, competition orientated machine, this is quite easy to achieve merely by transferring body weight to the rear of the machine and snapping open the throttle. Given a low gear, the front wheel should rise over any bumps or ridges less than a foot high and the rear wheel then follows quite easily. Try to tackle the same obstruction without lifting the front wheel and even with the best of front forks the result will be unpleasant. Key points to watch for are leaning too far back or pulling too hard on the handlebars, both of which could result in the wheel lifting too far. If this does happen, merely closing the throttle will bring everything under control again. The reverse is also true in that if the engine is not giving good power, thus causing the front end to lift, then no amount of tugging, pulling, heaving or weight transfer will get the front wheel up. First and most important, is to have the throttle open, and then transfer weight, and finally give a sharp tug at the handlebars.

On the trail, this trick will be essential for such manoeuvres as leaving a flooded or hazardous part of the track and cresting the ridge, which will run parallel, to gain access to the open countryside. Similarly, a steep rock ledge bridging a track can prove to be a real problem if torpedoed heavily, or a minor hindrance if the front wheel is lofted gracefully over it.

An allied skill is jumping the bike either uphill or down. The first thing to say is that jumping a cross-country bike is easy. Having said that, after mastering the art to your satisfaction, avoid it like the plague when trail riding. As soon as the bike leaves the ground, your control becomes lessened. It is possible to steer the bike in mid-air but this can only be done to a fine degree by a very good motocross rider or a world class enduro expert — and the enduro men at least, will rarely, if ever, be found using their skills. Further, unlike a motocross track, where one can be confident of the exact conditions prevailing in the chosen landing site, perhaps no more than 2-3 seconds will be available to assess the terrain prior to take off. That muddy patch the bike is going to plop into in a few moments time may be three inches deep or three feet, with a bottom of good firm gravel or sharp, loose stones. These problems of terrain already exist for the rider racing on an unseen natural track, without adding to them by prodigious leaps into the air.

However, on occasions, there is need for the bike to become airborne and as I have said, this poses no difficulty providing a little forethought is exercised. The golden rule, never to be broken on pain of ending up with a wet bottom, is to keep the throttle open on take off, whether jumping or downhill. To guarantee a successful landing, the front wheel must be higher than the rear on landing.

The same technique in actual use. The author floats the front wheel of his Bultaco Frontera over some ruts at high speed

In jumping uphill — for example cresting a ridge at speed on a steep climb — the body should be forward of the footrests so that on landing, the weight distribution is such that the bike does not loop. Ideally, the rear wheel should touch down just before the front, and done this way, a fifty mph landing can be achieved quite effortlessly. If too much weight is to the rear, then the throttle will have to be closed (effectively applying engine braking to the wheel) to bring the front end down and when it does hit the ground, the impact will be harder than is desirable. Also, the forward momentum of the bike will be slowed unnecessarily and this is bad.

Jumping on level ground should not occur in enduro riding except over ridges and again, the technique is simple. Throttle open on take-off, gentle tug on the 'bars and weight slightly rearward, and the bike will look after itself. However, I would re-iterate the need to avoid getting the bike airborne wherever possible. The fastest man is the one who keeps that rear wheel driving all the time, and also the one who takes the fewest risks.

Downhill jumps are the places where the ability to jump a bike is often invaluable, since these sections are the really time-consuming ones. Anyone can ride uphill at full bore but going down sorts the men from the boys (in this respect, I am very much a boy). The only modification in style required from the level jumping technique is that more weight needs to be transferred to the rear. Once you have landed front wheel first going downhill, you will never forget the experience, since you and the bike will almost certainly cartwheel for quite some distance, an instructive but not too pleasant experience.

The Frontera is a powerful racing machine and things can easily get out of hand. Here, Melling is trying to 'unwheelie'. That is, the sheer power of the 360cc engine has forced the front wheel to lift and the rider's weight has to be transferred well forward to bring the front wheel down without closing the throttle and losing momentum

Top left *All wrong! Too much weight to the rear of the bike has caused the bike to rise sharply and the MZ's very special style of unpredictable handling means that exciting things are about to happen to the rider*

Top right *This too, is all wrong! The bike is at far too sharp an angle and the rider is desperately trying to pull all his weight forward in order to bring the front end down. The situation was caused by an excessive amount of body weight on the rear of the machine at take off*

Right *Monty Python's answer to Evel Knievel. The author putting a factory 360cc Jawa through its paces and proving that a trail bike can be jumped just like a MX machine — and wishing he hadn't*

A perfectly executed uphill jump, neat, fast and quite effortless

Jumping on the flat, like all other jumps, should be avoided wherever possible. However, even a heavy bike, such as this Triumph, can be jumped with ease providing the throttle is kept open on take off

Failure to do this will result in a front wheel landing. Nasty, very nasty indeed!

Looking once again to motocross for riding techniques, it is useful to be able to broadslide an enduro bike. The classic occasion when this springs to mind is the inevitable drop down from a forest track on to a shale road. After one Welsh enduro, this section will become a familiar friend and the method to deal with it never changes. As the mud track finishes and the shale begins, lay the bike down and give a sharp tweak at the throttle at the same time as turning sharply. The rear wheel will step out of line in the direction the bike is turning. Roll the throttle back slightly and turn the handlebars into the slide. That is, in the same direction as the rear wheel is drifting. This will bring it back into line and as soon as the bike is in a straight line, full throttle can be applied. This is neat, effective and good fun.

The same sort of thing can be done on forestry tracks at high speed and it is quite possible to broadslide an enduro bike through shale bends in a most effective manner. The difference is that at 15mph — the speed at which mud track to shale road trick is likely to be attempted — things happen rather more slowly, and commensurately are more easily rectified, than if the speedometer needle is stuck at the 70mph mark. It is tempting to try sliding the bike on those gorgeous sweeping shale roads, but speaking from experience, I can say with hand on heart that shale is awfully hard if you hit it fast enough. Make haste slowly is a sound maxim.

Right at the other end of the speed scale, but equally difficult, are the very narrow uphill climbs that always seem to be just before a tight time check. These are usually no more than paths, some four to eight feet wide and can range from hub-deep mud, to polished stone. A good course plotter will bring the rider on to it unawares and from a difficult angle. On occasions, the gradient will be severe.

Because the track is so narrow and often obstructed by overhanging trees, it is difficult to go quickly on them. Speed, as we have already noted, is the essence of any successful climb. What is needed in such cases is a technique borrowed from the observed trials rider. Stand up on the footrests, select as high a gear as possible for maximum drive, and then gently keep the bike moving. Given a clear run, it is possible to traverse the majority of these tracks in this fashion, but on most occasions there will be some form of obstruction, normally in the form of a less fortunate rider, stuck, which will mean that you will have to slow down to such a speed where standing on the footrests is no longer practical.

Sit down on the saddle and paddle (effectively walking with one's legs whilst sitting on the bike) the machine round the obstacle. Then find some way of getting the bike up to a speed where a standing position can be resumed. This might entail leaving the best route up the track and using some virgin grass which still has good grip to offer, or riding at an angle to the track — anything at all is acceptable so that a standing position is regained. The reasons for this are twofold. First of all, the bike is infinitely more manoeuvrable when balanced between the rider's legs and can be snaked to and fro at will. Equally important is that riding this way consumes only moderate physical effort whereas paddling the bike is real torture. Not only will the rider be exhausted at the end of the climb, but he will be slower on the next section until he has got his breath back.

Such hazards will tax the rider's ability to choose terrain with good grip as much as anything else. Of the more obvious elements involved, avoiding ruts unless absolutely necessary, (and they often are) is paramount; closely followed by loose stones embedded in mud. Always try to seek out grass which has not been used, or alternatively, large areas of rock which have been scrubbed clean of their top covering of moss and mud. If you are trail riding for pleasure, then the virgin grass will be the most likely, and if competing, rocks, since unless you have an exceptionally early starting number, all the good grass will have long since been ploughed into a morass by your equally canny opponents.

Make your choice and then stick to it, come what may. Do not be afraid to open the throttle and ignore the bike's complaints just as long as you can keep it upright and heading in the right direction. The end result may be technically imperfect, but if you and the bike make it to the next section with the maximum speed and minimum effort, then nothing else matters.

This rule can be usefully extended to all forms of trail riding. Never be frightened of winding open the throttle, since a bike under power will claw its way out of the most incredible tangles. The worst that can happen is that you will fall off in a heap and since I have never heard of a trail rider being killed in action, even this cannot be too much of a threat. Make your decision and then DEMAND that the bike obey it, come what may. Faint heart never won fair lady nor kept on schedule in the ISCA 150.

Bogs are the one aspect of trail riding which I do not like. Mud, dust, rocks, rain, sleet and impossible gradients I relish as challenges to be met, conquered and enjoyed. Bogs I loathe and fear. The reason is simple. It is possible to ride hard and well for three hours and sixty miles and never make a mistake, only to come to grief in ten yards of morass. Bogs are unpredictable and can put a permanent end to a day's riding in a few seconds. Obviously, they need treating with care.

The classic descent from the woods on to a forestry track. The rider stands upright, with his weight well to the rear and just feathers the rear brake to steady his descent

On reaching the dirt road, the throttle is opened, the rider's left leg is used as a skid and the rear wheel slides out in a steady drift

Finally, the left leg can be put back on the footrest and since the bike is more or less in a straight line, can be accelerated hard. This manoeuvre is a lot of fun and not very much harder than it sounds

I am not an ISDT expert by any means and so my assessment of these nasty areas, you may think, is excessively pessimistic. This is fair comment, but bear in mind that even world class riders can get into trouble just as easily as novices. Swopping horror stories with Andy Roberton after the first day of the 1975 Welsh Two Day Trial — and a violently hard day it was too — I was surprised to find that he, a motocross rider of international status and previous outright winner of the Welsh, had fallen off attempting to traverse a bog. He had approached it in the time honoured fashion — fast, with plenty of power on tap — chosen a series of grassy hummocks to skip the bike across, and had suddenly found the front wheel disappearing in ooze. Andy reckoned he decelerated from 40mph to zero in about a yard. Apparently his flight over the handlebars was equally spectacular. The lesson from this incident is that bogs can mean trouble for any rider — regardless of skill or experience.

When approaching a bog, it is often worth stopping and having a good look round, even when riding competitively. A three minute survey could save fifteen minutes of really hard work as a result of driving in blindly. You will be looking for the narrowest part of the bog, preferably with gently sloping sides and a good supply of thick, matted hummocks. Danger areas will be smooth patches covered with moss or any obstacle such as a boulder, which might slow down one's exit.

At this juncture, it is useful if we understand just what lies beneath a trail bog. Few organisers, at least those who have ever done any riding themselves, will ever send riders out into marshland, and no trail rider with a modicum of sense would ever stray into these regions of his own volition. The expedition could well be fatal — literally. What we are considering are streams whose valleys cross a track and which have gradually filled up with material. This debris can range from virtually liquid consistency to quite solid, and the surface of the bog will have the same range of conditions. For a moment, let us empty the bog and substitute a stream.

The stream has a valley formed in the rock and this has to be ridden down on entry and up on exit. Now if we fill in the valley with bog again, the topography will change but the rock sides of the valley will still exist. So will the stream bed — and this piece of information is vital.

Although I am not prepared to be even slightly dogmatic about riding bogs, I prefer the fast entry technique rather than the finesse some riders display. This involves hitting the bog as fast as possible using a high gear, ear, with the engine pulling hard. The bike's momentum will then carry you some considerable distance before anything else happens. Try to choose a crossing which is narrow, and make use of any hummocks, since these will easily carry the weight of the rider and bike. With speed, confidence and a touch of luck, most bogs can be traversed in this manner. However, it is essential to know PRECISELY where the bike is supposed to go and just how fast the approach run can be made. Hence the need for the reconnaissance trip. An expert rider can survey the scene as he rides up to it — a lesser mortal needs to do the job on foot.

Unfortunately, some bogs are just too wide to be jumped and what often happens is that the front wheel starts to sink and hits the submerged bank of the valley. Not surprisingly, since the bank is part of some billions of tons of rock, the machine stops quickly. There are now two alternatives. First, quietly commit suicide by strangling yourself with a spare inner tube, or two, think your way out of the situation. I prefer number two, even though a certain degree of willpower is needed to avoid screaming at the sight of your shiny new £800 bike sinking into oblivion.

Get off the bike and feel the bog's bank, in front of you. Very often it is a matter of inches away and on many occasions, the front wheel will make it, leaving the back stranded. If the bank is near, rock the bike to and fro to loosen it and then slowly drag first the front and then the rear on firmer ground. It is always easier to pull the bike sideways out of the mud, rather than forward or back, since the machine can then be laid down on its side in the bog. In this way, the bike's weight is spread over a greater area and hence is less likely to sink. At this juncture, let me say that it is far easier to write about extricating a bog-bound bike than it is to actually do it. However, faced with the inevitable, it must be done and there is no way out.

Let me digress slightly by saying that will-power, not muscle power, is the key to escape. The rider must say to himself, "I WILL get the bike out and continue riding and nothing is going to stop me." Once the slightest hint of defeat creeps into the mind then the job becomes as good as impossible.

The worst cases are where the bog is just too big to blast across, and as the machine loses momentum, it just churns into the morass. Once stopped, do not continue to spin the rear wheel, since this will only increase the depth of the slot cut into the mud. Get off the bike and pull the front wheel out of the mire and on to anything which is even just a little bit firmer. Then do the same with the rear. To have any hope of escape, the rear wheel must be placed on something which will give it some chance to drive. A hummock, or stone outcrop, or even some virgin bog — anything at all, even if it means manhandling the bike a few yards. Start the motor and engage first or second gear, second being the better if the motor will pull well, but do not sit on the bike. Let out the clutch and give the bike a shove forward at the same time and then run alongside it as it moves. With any luck —

The dreaded bogs! Hazard even to the best of riders

The author's own preference for attacking bogs is one which relies on speed and brute force rather than finesse

all bog exercises need this — the riderless bike will be light enough to skate to safety, dragging its exhausted rider after it.

Just one word of warning. Do not be tempted, through something as inconsequential as utter exhaustion, for example, to stop taking the bike for a walk, until you are absolutely positive of being on firm ground. I have seen a number of riders rescue their bikes and make good progress towards dry ground, only to give up just a few yards from the end, and have the situation revert to square one. Nasty, very nasty indeed.

In an enduro, if the bog is a bad one, there will be quite a number of riders struggling. The first thing to do, is note their position and avoid them. Instead, study the laconic ISDT rider (there is always one about) who deviates 50 yards from the track and crosses without getting his wheel rims dirty. If you too manage to emulate your brothers, and get stuck, then try and strike a bargain with a neighbour and you can both get on your way. You help him and he helps you. And stick to it, for anyone who welches on such a deal wants nailing to a pine tree as a course marker. Thinking about it, that might well happen if you double-cross some of the sport's more volatile members.

On occasions, there can be humorous sides to the bog rescue business. In the following year's Welsh, I was having a good ride and had not made one mistake regarding bogs in 300 miles. Then, on the afternoon of the last day, a fine drizzle began to fall which made it difficult to see through one's goggles. Momentarily distracted by this nuisance, I struggled to pull down my goggles and smartly plopped the bike into a real morass. Almost instantly, it began to sink and with it my hopes of a medal.

Just then, like the fairy Godmother, who should arrive on the scene but Bob Perrin, clerk of the course for the Beacons Enduro, and two other members of the Welsh Trail Riders Association, following the course as spectators. Bob and I had been having a rather heated public debate regarding the severity and organization of the Beacons Enduro and the look on his face when he saw his arch critic firmly trapped was one of pure rapture. His first comment was a long sigh followed by "I wish I had a camera!". Then without further discussion, the four of us set to work on the bike and in 30 seconds, it was safely parked on terra firma. The fact that four fit and strong men were needed to move it indicates the severity of the problem and just how much my precious medal was jeopardized. More important, it also shows what thoroughly good sorts are involved in the trial riding world, for the degree of sportsmanship that Bob Perrin showed is extremely rare today.

Water crossings which are fully liquid, rather than sticky and evil, are no real problem at all, providing the water is not too deep. Stand on the footrests, select a low gear, and keep the motor revving well — then guide the bike through the stream, river or whatever just as you would do on dry land, and if it cannot be seen, assume the worst. If the stream bed is gravel, it can be ridden just like a motorway, but if it is composed of large, loose rocks, then more care will be needed. The water itself will have no effect on the bike other than to slow it down at high speeds.

Water crossings which are fully liquid, rather than sticky and evil, are no real problem at all, providing the water is not too deep. Stand on the footrests, select a low gear, and keep the motor revving well — then guide the bike through the stream, river or whatever just as you would do on dry land, and if it can't be seen, assume the worst. If the stream bed is gravel, it can be ridden just like a motorway, but if it is composed of large, loose rocks, then more care will be needed. The water itself will have no effect on the bike other than to slow it down at high speeds.

The biggest dangers are rushing in spectacularly and creating such a big bow wave that the motor drowns. If this happens, it serves you right and I have no sympathy whatsoever. A lesser danger is finding an underwater pothole which will submerge the machine entirely. A good, well-prepared trail bike will operate quite happily with the cylinder head at water level and for short periods, submerged. Providing water does not get in through the air-filter, or sucked up the exhaust pipe by the back pressure, modern electrics will function quite happily under water. I can vouch for this from practical experience. Plenty of revs from the engine, whilst still maintaining a slow forward motion, will keep the exhaust system free of water and sound preparation should take care of the induction side. However, even the best prepared and carefully ridden bike is going to give up if pressed to ridiculous ends — such as tank deep water — and then the rider must quickly exercise his judgement. As soon as the situation becomes hopeless, shut the throttle and stop the bike. If this is done promptly, then no damage will result and the bike can be dragged or pushed to dry land and started again without too much trouble. The danger lies in water entering the combustion chamber. Should this happen, there is a good chance that the con-rod will bend or the cylinder head crack for since water is incompressible, all sorts of nasty things can happen when the piston tries to achieve the impossible on its way up the bore.

When riding in an enduro, have a good look round before crossing a river, if it looks at all suspicious. For

The sensible approach to water crossings. A low gear, high engine revs and relatively low approach speed are used. It will be found that a well-prepared bike can easily deal with 3-4 feet of water if tackled in this way

The silly approach to the same crossing. Very spectacular, but foolish in the extreme. Not only are bike and rider thoroughly drowned but the risk of hitting a pothole or other submerged obstacle at a speed which would almost certainly result in a fall, is much increased

example, if there are half a dozen dead bikes littered around, it pays to get off the bike and find out where they went wrong before you plunge in. I have seen international riders do just this when they were unsure, so the beginner has every justification for a recce.

Executed competently, the techniques described so far should take the rider well up to the level of the clubman enduro rider or a Grade "A" green lane explorer. However, no doubt there will be some zealots who will want to press their skills further and for those enthusiasts the following section is included.

The first party trick is one which can be used by trail riders as well as enduroists, although it will only be the braver souls who will find a need for it. The normal method for riding downhill is to select low gear, apply both brakes until they are just on the point of locking and then stand up with plenty of weight to the rear and ride the bike down. If the hill is long and steep, it often pays to ride across it like a slalom skier, in order to keep the bike's speed down to manageable proportions. 99.9% of all descents can be managed in this fashion. Once in a thousand miles, a real killer occurs.

This sort of hill is so steep that to ride down it would be dangerous or perhaps the surface is too loose for any real braking to be effected. In this case, get off the bike and gently ease the front wheel over, then bring the rear in line so that the bike is at 90° to the line of descent. Then, taking care to stand uphill of the bike, lift it slightly so that only the tyres are in contact with the ground. At this point, it will start to slide away (if it doesn't, then this hill is not steep enough to warrant the manoeuvre). To regulate your speed, lie the bike down so that the footrests, rear wheel spindle and handlebars bite into the ground. In this way, almost anything short of a vertical cliff face can be conquered. It's not neat, nor is it easy, but it will get you down. If by any chance the bike does start to slide down, then for goodness sake, let it go. New bikes are easy to obtain — replacement bodies are in somewhat shorter supply.

Earlier in the chapter, we looked at the advantages of broadsliding a bike, particularly on shale. It is worth remembering that the same technique can be used wherever there is a need to make a turn quickly. For example, sometimes a dirt road joins a tarmaced track and it is helpful if the bike can be aimed in a straight line with the minimum of fuss. Even in dry weather, the dust on the tyres will be sufficient to break traction on the tarmac, if the machine is accelerated hard. Of course, this sort of riding must only be employed in enduros, where the tarmac track is owned by the Forestry Commission, or a private landowner, for on the public roads not only would it be dangerous but it would also do positive damage to trail riding's image in the public eye.

If traction is broken with only dust to help, then it takes little imagination to see that when tarmac is wet, or has mud carried on to it by the passage of bikes, then it becomes very slippery. Some riders live in fear of going quickly on wet or muddy tarmac but tackled sensibly, it is no harder to deal with than any other terrain. The difficulty with tarmac is that it is very easy to go quickly on it, even in the wet, and this can lead the unwary rider into travelling at higher speeds than he can safely manage. Treat the surface as wet grass and you will be erring on the right side and remember that whilst a modern knobbly tyre can be used almost like any normal tyre on dry tarmac, its wet-weather properties are still poor. It will tend to lose its grip quite suddenly and the resultant slide is often vicious and more difficult to correct than if the same thing happened on the rough.

Some of the climbs in Enduros can be steep enough to tax even a good competition bike and a skilful rider. It is of paramount importance to keep up a reasonable speed and this can be difficult if the track is very steep or has hairpin bends. A trick gleaned from the MotoCross world is to use the earth banking as a wall of death and ridden this way, it is often possible to negotiate a corner without backing off the throttle. It will be obvious as you ride up to the section whether or not it is possible to adopt this method, for what is needed is some form of banking on the outside of the corner against which the bike's wheels can be driven. This need not be too big for in MotoCross; the groove formed by the passage of the machines on a smooth grass corner will be ample for the riders to use. However, in an enduro, it is better to be safe than spectacular, so ensure that there is a substantial bank against which the bike can be ridden. Getting round is then only a matter of keeping the throttle hard open and having the confidence to lay the bike over to what might seem a dangerous angle. In fact, if the banking is ideal, the machine can be leaned over until it is almost parallel with the ground, since centrifugal force will keep it firmly attached to the bank. I would hasten to add that this degree of skill and confidence is the province of the experts.

In addition to keeping speed up for climbs, the same technique can be used in reverse, on fast descents, particularly if you have misjudged your speed. It is very useful to be able to slam your bike into a banked hairpin and so both negotiate the corner quickly and at the same time lose speed. At the risk of stating the obvious, don't attempt either of these tricks on the trail before you have practised them and certainly never, ever, attempt them in an enduro until you can be sure of completing them successfully.

Banking can also be very useful on the fast shale roads in the forestry, as Andy Roberton showed me in the 1976 Welsh International Two Day Trial. I had always thought that the fastest way through the forestry roads was to broadside the bike through corners in the style epitomized by ISDT aces, like Ernie Page. However, after being passed by the canny Welshman repeatedly throughout the trial, (Andy·started just behind me and so being faster got to every check with ample time to spare, whilst I just scraped home), I am beginning to have second thoughts.

Roberton's method is to dive deep on to the cambered edge on the inside of the corner of the shale road, using the banking just as I have described. This allows maximum power to be used, without any fear of the rear wheel stepping out. The bike then shoots across the loose shale in the centre of the road, more or less in a straight line. Crossing the loose stuff will cause it to wiggle and shake, but providing there is sufficient speed, there will be no trouble. The bike can be then aimed at the next cambered bank and the manoeuvre repeated.

Personally, I find this a much more relaxing method than playing at Speedway and it seems just as quick. What is sure, is that it is a much less tiring style and this in itself can be a great advantage during a long event. The only danger I can foresee for the less than expert rider is hitting the bank too slowly and sliding down one of the drainage ditches in the process. Not, I would think, an experience to be repeated twice.

With a really desperate descent, this is one way of getting a bike and rider down more or less in one piece. First steer the bike across the slope, slowing its progress by using the front brake. When it begins to gain momentum, and there is a danger of it running away, drop the handlebars and footrests into the earth and this should stop it. Then begin the descent again, running across the camber. Since any slope less than 1:1 should present no problem at all, this technique should be reserved only for real precipices such as are found in the major enduros

9 It's a clean machine*

With apologies to The Beatles

Because a trail bike is used under more arduous conditions than a normal motorcycle, it will require more care and attention if it is to function effectively.

A machine which is prepared well initially, and ridden with some sympathy, will usually give many hundreds, if not thousands, of miles of trouble free riding, provided it is maintained regularly.

To give a maintenance scheme for every trail bike in Britain, or even the more popular marques, would be a mammoth task and certainly one far beyond the scope of this book. Instead, I propose to look at some general areas of maintenance which are common to most bikes.

The worst thing about trail riding for me is that my nice clean bike comes back covered in mud. So the first job after every outing must be to get the bike into a sufficiently clean state for it to be checked over and prepared ready for the next run.

First of all, wash the heavy mud off the bike with a hosepipe. A good strong jet of water will soon shift all the muck but beware of high pressure systems which can actually force water through engine case joints, or even into the cylinder on a two-stroke. My CCM-engined motocross machine is not even slightly waterproof and a hosepipe directed at the engine will easily penetrate both the rocker box, gearbox and primary chain covers. For the same reason, avoid aiming the jet of water directly at either the carburettor or any part of the electrical system.

Having removed the heavy dirt, give the bike a good scrub off with a bucket of very soapy, hot water. I use a squeeze of dish washing liquid of sufficient quantity to elicit a howl of annoyance at the cost from my wife, in two gallons of near boiling water. The bike is then given a thorough cleaning, using a stiff brush for the frame, rear suspension units and any other steel parts; a long-handled dish washing brush with softer bristles for the aluminium bits, and a damp rag for the petrol tank and the few parts of the bike which have a glossy finish.

Finally, lightly hose the suds off the bike and like Cinderella at the ball, your muddy motorcycle will re-appear in all its former glory.

If it is possible, take the bike out for a short run immediately after washing, so that the engine can be dried off and you can confirm that water has not found its way into the carburettor or electrics. At the same time, half a dozen hard applications of the brakes will dry them out.

If the ride has been an easy one, then all that will be needed before the bike is re-used is to check the condition of the chain and adjust and lubricate it. This is a ceaseless chore for all trail riders except those fortunate few who are blessed, and this is not too strong a term, with fully enclosed rear chains.

Possibly the greatest step forward in the protection of exposed chain was the introduction of Duckhams Chain and is, in my opinion, the finest chain lubricant in the world. When we first began using it in the Fantic team, we literally doubled the life of the chains on all three machines — a result I would never have believed unless I had witnessed it with my own eyes.

At one time, the chain had to be removed from the bike after every ride and first washed in paraffin and then boiled in high melting point grease — a system which was instrumental in more than one divorce, since kitchen stoves, whilst ideal for boiling chains, are not enhanced by blobs of black grease being liberally sprayed about their enamel coats. Now, unless the chain has had a very bad time — for example a long ride through liquid mud — all that is needed is to wipe off the top layer of dust and give the inside of the rollers a good spray with the yellow foam which comprises the lubricant. This foam penetrates the rollers as a liquid and then sets, if this is a

First stage in cleaning the bike is to protect any vulnerable parts, such as the carburettor or electrical system, from being hit directly by a jet of water

Then give the bike a thorough soaking. This will remove the less stubborn lumps of mud and weaken the resolve of the troublecausers

Next, give the whole bike a vigorous scrub

Finally, a hose down will bring the bike up to pristine condition. Unfortunately, this series of operations has to be repeated several times if the bike is really muddy and in this case, the final stage should be a wash with hot soapy water, followed by a hosing down

sufficiently accurate term to describe the way the liquid hardens, into a sticky grease with quite remarkable powers of adhesion. Used directly after washing, not only will the chain be prevented from rusting but when the bike is taken out later, the lubricant will have penetrated and hardened.

In dusty weather, the air-filter will need regular attention if the engine is to give good performance. Many bikes are fitted with foam filters and whilst these are extremely good at filtering dust, as a natural consequence of their effectiveness, they become easily blocked.

After removing from the air-filter box, the thick mass of oil and dust should be washed off the filter, with petrol. The filter can then be thoroughly cleansed by washing in hot water with yet another liberal dose of washing-up liquid, since this is just as good as using petrol, but much cheaper.

When the filter is clean, soak it in a clean SAE 30 oil and then squeeze it very hard, until apparently all the oil has been removed. These elements filter by encouraging the dust to adhere to the sticky surface of the oil. This surface needs only to be thousandths of an inch thick to be effective, for if there is too much present, the oil will actually clog the tiny pores of the filter.

After liberally greasing the face of the filter which meets the air-filter box, the element can be replaced. Although making the task of cleaning the filter element much more difficult, the layer of grease serves two important functions. Firstly, it seals the joint against dust. Secondly, and more importantly, it makes the ingress of water more difficult. Foam filters are very susceptible to water permeation since the liquid can flow quite happily through the pores. If there is a gap between the element and the filter box — even a tiny one — the film of oil will prevent the passage of dust but will not stop water. With this in mind, I always grease the element thoroughly and whilst this does not guarantee that water will not work its way through, it does increase the degree of protection.

The author's Crooks Suzuki after the 1976 ISCA 150. The event was a tough one!

After an event like the ISCA, the bike has to be thoroughly cleaned and checked in order to ensure its continued reliability. Both wheels have been removed, as has the air filter element. The electrical system has been checked, and the chain cleaned and re-oiled. Whilst the bike is in this state, it can be thoroughly examined for any wear or damage

If your bike has a paper filter element, it will fare much better in very wet conditions because the paper will absorb the moisture to quite a surprising degree. When dusty, they can be cleaned by blowing from the inside with a high pressure air-line: a friendly garage is an essential for this exercise. Although not encouraged by manufacturers, since it is supposed to wash out the element's impregnation, they can also be washed in the traditional bucket of hot water with a liberal squeeze of soap. Although in theory this is inadvisable, in practice it does seem to work and one could be forgiven if one imagined that manufacturers had an interest in seeing filters renewed rather than cleaned.

Depending on how the bike has been used (whether a gentle or hard ride) and on the type of terrain encountered, then the tyres should be checked for cuts and also see if the tubes have moved to such an extent that there is a chance of the valve stem being torn out. Such remedial action as is necessary, taken in the comfort of a dry workshop, is far better than a struggle out on the moors, with dusk fast approaching.

In addition to lubricating, oils on a competition machine also act as filters. I change the engine oil on my CCM motocross machine every single meeting and more than save the cost of the lubricant in a reduced spare parts bill. Owners of four stroke machines would be well advised to take similar precautions and oil changes at no more than 500 miles, at a maximum, are to be strongly recommended for any bike used regularly on the rough.

The gearbox oil fares much better, but even so a surprising amount of debris finds its way into the lubricant. For this reason, I change this oil, whether on a two-stroke or four-stroke machine, every 500 miles.

Because I am changing front fork oils very regularly to suit differing weather conditions and in an effort to continually improve my machine's handling, I never have a specified interval for draining. However, for the average rider, it would be a sensible proposition to change the gearbox and front fork oils and, if not serviced

These grooves around the edge of the brake plate help prevent the ingress of mud and water as well as assisting cooling. They should be periodically cleaned out with a toothbrush

The inside of the hub should be given similar treatment and then wiped out with a clean, petrol-soaked rag

Finally, the brake shoes should be removed and cleaned and the brake cam and pivot lightly greased. They can be most easily re-fitted as shown

previously, wash the air-filter every 500 miles. This may be erring slightly on the side of over-maintenance but far better to change lubricants early and have perfectly clean air-filters, than ruin an expensive motorcycle by having contaminated oil and a filthy air-filter.

If the ride has been a hard one, then it is as well to remove the wheels and clean out the dust and mud which will have worked its way into the hubs. This job will often vary from bike to bike but there are one or two universal tips.

Wash the wheel spindle and any retaining nuts or studs in petrol and lightly grease them before reassembling the rear wheel. Be particularly careful not to over-grease the wheel spindle, since any excess could well find its way onto the brake shoes, thus rendering the brake almost useless. In use, the greased nuts and studs will become covered in muck and look absolutely filthy. But they will come off beautifully next time the wheel is stripped. Assemble them dry, allow for the ingress of water and then try to remove a pinch bolt which has not been disturbed for four or five months. The task will be a challenging one.

When the brake plate has been removed from the hub, thoroughly clean the brake liner with a petrol soaked rag and then remove any traces of petrol with a perfectly dry piece of kitchen tissue. This seems to prevent the liner from acquiring a layer of muddy, grease-impregnated filth, which seems peculiar to bikes used on the rough.

The better designed brakes have a lip on the plate which slots inside a groove machined into the hub. This acts as a seal and helps reduce the amount of water which gets into the hub. Very often, this groove becomes blocked with mud and cannot function effectively. An old toothbrush is ideal for removing the dirt found here.

If water has caused corrosion of any of the brake internals and they have to be stripped and cleaned, do not over-grease them, for a brake hub can get very hot and we have already discussed the dangers of grease on the brake linings. Having given this warning, not greasing the parts is just as bad, for a stud which has welded itself electrolytically to an aluminium casting is almost impossible to remove, without damage to one part or the other.

Finally, as a matter of policy, the whole bike should be given a careful check after every ride. Correcting a loose nut or an air-filter hose which is beginning to split can save pounds in repair bills and prevent a good day's riding being ruined.

The adage, 'prevention is better than cure', cannot be too highly stressed in this case.

Applying the enduroist's chain panacea — Duckham's Chain Lube

Hard, fast and demanding — and also some of the best fun in the two-wheel world — that's enduros

10 They said it was just a fast trail ride

Trail riding is a non-competitive pastime, an activity where pleasure comes from taking part, rather than achieving any degree of sporting success. The best ride imaginable could well be an amble along some quiet, grassy track on an autumn evening, or it could be a fifty mile broadslide through a Welsh forest. To me, the latter is trail riding at its best; to many other riders, the thought of racing along tracks which could be savoured at a more leisurely pace is anathema. I don't wish to condemn the green lane ramblers' idea of trail riding, or even criticise it. However, there are a lot of riders who enjoy pitting their skills at riding and machine preparation against the wiles of an organiser in an extended trail ride which will, in its best form, test the bike and rider to the limits of endurance. For this ever-increasing band of riders, I include the next two Chapters.

An enduro, even a poor one, will give the opportunity to ride more miles of tracks and rough lanes than all but the most diligent and determined rider could cram into a normal day's trail riding. In Britain's premier event, the International Welsh Two-Day trial, competitors are asked to drive about 180 miles during each of the two days, of which roughly 120 miles will be on unmade tracks, moorland and similar terrain. That is the equivalent of travelling from Liverpool to London in one day on a trail bike, and without using any tarmac roads except those covering the distance from the outskirts of each city to the centre.

The Beacons and ISCA 150 events have shorter mileage — a mere hundred miles a day — but this is composed entirely of rough going. Even a minor event will give the rider the opportunity to tackle 50 or 60 miles of tracks, which is as much as a good day's trail riding.

In addition to the distance covered, some parts of the route, and again this varies according to the severity of the event, will be much harder than most riders are used to attempting. Sometimes an organiser suffers from megalomania and includes a section which is beyond the capabilities of almost all the entry, which results in a lot of cursing and threats to bring down death and disaster on the perpetrator of the pain and suffering. But everything gets sorted out in the end and most riders grin and bear it in a sportsmanlike fashion — then sneak off at the end of the event and let down the tyres on the clerk of the course's car.

The average trail rider has two new problems in an enduro — distance and severity — but there is also the vital third element which gives the event its piquancy — speed! Not only does the enduroist have to ride further and over harder terrain than his green lane counterpart, but he also has to ride faster. Further, faster, harder — three factors which together combine to present a real challenge.

Enduros are still an embryo sport in Britain, where almost every form of motorcycle competition flourishes. These events used to be called reliability trials and the name enduros, imported from America, has recently come into favour in order to distinguish the events we are discussing, in which the main element of competition is speed, from observation trials, which usually place maximum emphasis on a rider's ability to negotiate difficult sections of terrain without putting his feet down. Unfortunately, some observed trials have a speed element in them, such as the famous Scott Trial in Yorkshire, but are not enduros, and some enduros are called trials, such as the Welsh Two Day, but do not have any observed sections. However, the trend is more than ever to call long distance reliability events, where the rider has to arrive at several checkpoints at a specified time, enduros; and observed trials, trials. By 1995, things should be just nicely clarified.

There are not a lot of enduros in Britain, when compared with the number of events in the motorcycling field and for this reason, there has yet to appear any accepted method of organisation, scoring or entry. This can be fun in that one event is radically different from another but basically they revolve around the system used

CAERLEON MOTORSPORTS CLUB

SUPPLEMENTARY REGULATIONS

ISCA 150

22 FEBRUARY 1976

A Regional Restricted Trial held under the General Competition Rules (10th edition) of the Auto Cycle Union and Standing Trials Regulations (1966) together with these Supplementary Regulations (1966) and any further instruction that may be issued. The event is open to members of Clubs in all the Welsh Centres, and by invitation to members of the Services Clubs riding 'solo' motor cycles.

R.A.C. Permit Applied For
A.C.U. Permit Applied For

-1-

OFFICIALS

A.C.U. Steward	-	As Appointed
Club Steward	-	
Machine Examiner	-	
Paddock Marshall	-	
Clerk of the Course	-	P. Winchester
Secretary of Meeting	-	G.M. Jenkins
		21 Sycamore Court
		Woodfield Park
		Blackwood
		Gwent

Entries close on 25 January 1976

-2-

START & FINISH

Will be at:
First man away 09.31 a.m.
Riders will start in pairs.
Machines to be in closed control 30 minutes before starting time.

ENTRIES

Entries and Team nominations must be in the hands of the Secretary of the Meeting by 25 January 1976.
Entries will be limited to first 150 received.
Drivers have the choice of riding under two speed schedules.

A - Clubmans
B - Expert

and must indicate on the entry form which class they wish to enter.
Drivers will not be allowed to change classes.

TEAMS

Each Team shall consist of 3 riders already entered individually. No Rider may ride for more than one Team.

-3-

ENTRY FEE

Not returnable unless trial is cancelled.

Individual Entry	--	£5.00
Team Entry Club	--	£2.00
Team Entry Trade	--	£4.00
Team Entry One Make	--	£4.00

The Organisers reserve the right to refuse entry, without explanation (subject to S.R.4)

EXAMINATIONS

Machines must be presented for Examination in numerical order, 1 hour before starting time and must be in closed control 30 minutes before starting time.

-4-

AWARDS

PREMIER	)	
Best 175cc	)	'B' Schedule only
Best over 175cc	)	
Best Clubman	)	
Best 175cc	)	'A' Schedule only
Best over 175cc	)	
Best Services Rider	)	'A' or 'B' Schedule
Best Club Team	)	
Best Trade Team	)	Subject to 3 Teams
Best One Make Team	)	
Best Services Team	)	

No driver may take more than one open award.

MEDALS

For the purpose of this event medals will be awarded based on the best performance in the Expert and Clubmans Classes.

GOLD

These will be awarded to all drivers with a total number of points not exceeding by more than 15% the number of points received by the first driver of that Class. (Expert of Clubman).

SILVER

These will be awarded to all drivers with a total number of points not exceeding by more than 65% the number of points received by the first driver of that Class. (Expert or Clubman).

-5-

BRONZE

These will be awarded to all drivers who complete the Trial within the maximum time.

NATURE OF TRIAL

The course will consist of approximately 100 mls of Forestry and Moorland Tracks and other terrain, most of which will be in forests in the Brechfa area. Driving over a marked course to a specified time schedule with penalties for being late at the Time Checks. Performing a number of Special Tests, with points awarded according to time taken. The Special Tests will also be used to eliminate ties for any awards.

TIME CHECKS

The time allowed between checks will depend on the class of the track and nature of the terrain, but will always be in proportion between the following groups:-

"A" (All Capacities) 20 m.p.h.
"B" (All Capacities) 25 m.p.h.

(1) The position of the checks will be indicated by a white flag at 200 yds and a yellow flag at 20 yds before the Check Point. Except at the finish drivers must not pass the yellow flag until they are due to check in. (Penalty 20 points added).

(2) On reaching a Check a driver must immediately hand in his Time Card to the Check Controller. The card will be filled in and returned to the driver.

-6-

(3) Drivers will be allowed two minutes late at a Time Check without penalty but will lose one mark for every complete minute they are late beyond that allowance.

(4) A driver who is late at a Time Check is not allowed another two minutes, unless he gets back on to his original schedule.

(5) A driver may make up all or part of the time late if he so desires.

(6) Any rider more than 60 minutes late - excluding official delay - will deemed to have retired. Any driver passed by the Course Closing Marshal must leave the route and return to the Finish.

ROUTE CHECKS

These will be marked with a blue flag, drivers will get their Time Card stamped to prove passage, missing a route check will mean exclusion.

CONTROLS

Machines will be in control before the start of the trial, and immediately after clocking in at the end of each days run.

NO WORK OF ANY DESCRIPTION, INCLUDING REFUELING, WILL BE ALLOWED ON MACHINES WHILST IN CONTROL. (Penalty exclusion).

-7-

At the initial start each day, fifteen minutes before a driver is due to start, his number will be called, he will be admitted and will wheel his machine to the entrance of the working area and may work on his machine. Drivers are not allowed to use any tools other than those carried on the machine throughout the trial and are subject to the Closed Control regulations and penalties enclosed.

Refueling is not allowed in the closed control (Parc Ferme) but is permitted in the working area.

START

On being given the signal to start each day the engine must be started by the kick starter or the self starter and the machine driven over the second line, 20 metres from the start, within 1 minute, penalty for failure to start, 50 pts.

SPECIAL TESTS

There will be two special tests, one cross-country and one hill-climb. Duration of cross-country approximately 3½ miles, hill-climb approximately 1 mile. There will also be an acceleration test.

-8-

PENALTY POINTS

These will be debited to drivers on the following scale.

Late arrival at a check point per min.	60 pts
Entering closed control with running engine, working on machines between time check and closed control.	60 pts
Smoking or throwing things away in closed control.	5 pts
Starting engines in the working area.	300 pts
Using tools other than those carried on the machine throughout the trial.	300 pts
Working on the machine in the 'starting area' before the signal is given.	50 pts
Starting the engine before the starting signal has been given.	50 pts
Failure to start with starter provided within one minute of the signal being given.	50 pts
Losing time card.	10 pts
Early arrival at time clock, per min.	60 pts
Uncompleted day for team member.	15,000 pts
Special Tests, Hill Climb & Cross Country, each second.	1 pt
Acceleration, each second.	5 pts

-9-

GENERAL

All machines and drivers must satisfy legal requirements for use on the highway, any machine which is fitted with a suspect silencer will be tested by the Machine Examiner before being allowed to start, and excluded if it does not meet requirements. On the rough drivers must give way to walkers, horse riders, farm traffic, etc. All machines must be equipped with stands. Motor Cycle crash helmets must be worn at all times. Tyres optional. Number plates must be provided by the driver. One on the front and one on each side of the machine. Regulation size, oval (11½ x 9½) painted matt yellow with black 6 inch numbers. Marking will be by dayglo arrows.

-10-

Regulations for the 1975 ISCA 150 enduro

in the International Six Days Trial — or, as it is known throughout the motorcycling world — the ISDT.

This event was first held in 1913 and is the premier enduro in the world, being held for six days continuously over ultra-tough terrain and demanding extremely high speed schedules from the riders. It is a great privilege even to ride in this event and to win any medal is the achievement of a lifetime. Should you ever meet a rider who has won a Gold Medal — the highest award possible — then be aware that you are looking at one of the very, very best cross-country riders in the world.

The day starts off for each pair of riders at a given time, according to his capacity class. The smaller displacement machines start first and the biggest, last which is a convenient way of beginning the event and a reminder of the days when the big bikes were the fastest and the little 'uns struggled. This is no longer the case.

The rider has to kickstart the machine and ride it, under its own power, across a line 20 metres from the start. After this point he is deemed to have started and can get on with the event. However, if the bike will not start on the kickstart — and this is not always easy if the machine in question is a highly tuned racing motor — then the rider has to push his bike across the line and make what attempts he can to start the bike without assistance. This usually means a push and, as in the case of the 1975 Beacons enduro, if the start is uphill, the push will be uphill and this can be extremely exhausting. Rule number one for the novice enduro rider must be to ensure that his bike WILL start on demand. If you do have to resort to a push, you will be immediately debted 50 marks, which is a rather depressing start to the day's activities. Everyone will eventually get away.

In the ISDT, and the better British enduros, the course will be marked from then on and all that the rider has to do is follow it. In the ISDT, not only is the correct course marked but any alternatives are also marked with "NO ENTRY" signs so there can be no possible chance of making a mistake. Again, the best British events use this system.

A few enduros use a route card system, which is both ineffective and dangerous, since a rider cannot both navigate and race at the same time — but fortunately these are few and becoming less all the time.

About every twenty miles will be a check, at which point a record will be made of the rider's progress. There will be a clock visible on the table and when the time shown corresponds with that on his time card, the rider will approach the control zone, hand in his card to have the time recorded, and then progress to the next check.

He is not allowed to pass through the check before the time specified and if possible, must not arrive late either. The speeds that are required of a rider vary according to the event, but for a clubman, 20mph is usual. The experienced rider will try to go just slightly faster than this so that he arrives at the check five minutes early and has had time to clean his goggles, check his bike over and have a mental and physical rest before setting out once more. This is easy to write, but often difficult to achieve and on many occasions riders will scream into a check, thrust their time cards at the official and roar away without even stopping their engines. This is the time to discover whether your bike can take the CONTINUOUS flat out trail riding at a speed almost as fast as motocross.

In a good event, you will have to ride hard all the time in order to avoid penalties for lateness, but the idea should be to ride as slowly as possible and still arrive at your specified time. The slower the pace, the easier it is to finish in an enduro. And that means riding the last mile just as quickly as the first. Other than impressing the spectators, it is of little use setting a blazing pace for the first 75 miles only to wear the bike out in the final section. As in any racing, there are no prizes for the man who nearly wins — only for the one who actually does.

After two or three timed sections, when a competent rider should be able to keep on time and maintain a clean sheet (ie. having incurred no penalties), there will come a speed, or cross-country test. This can be composed of a timed section amounting to only half a mile, or quite a lengthy run over three-quarters of an hour. The best ones are of three or four miles in length — a distance which is sufficiently short to allow the rider to go flat out all the time and yet long enough for one error of judgement not to ruin the rider's time.

The fastest rider over the speed test will score zero marks and all the riders in the trial (or class, depending on the organisation) will accrue marks at the rate of 1 per second for the difference between their time and the man who sets standard time. These marks will then be added to the rider's on-going total for lateness penalties and at the end of the trail, the talented individual who has LEAST marks, will have won the event.

Overall winners in an enduro are normally awarded a trophy or cup, but never, to the best of my knowledge, cash, since fortunately, this element has not yet crept into the sport. Other riders are then awarded Gold, Silver or Bronze medals depending on what percentage of the winner's score they managed to achieve. For example, if the winner lost 100 marks, Golds will be received by all riders who scored between 101 and 115 (winner's marks plus 15%); Silver winners would need 116 - 165 (winner's total plus 65%) and all other official finishers would receive a Bronze medal.

By the time you are winning anything other than a Bronze medal, you will be in a position to write your own book about enduros, for none of the three medals are easy to obtain in one of the big events and very few are awarded at each meeting.

The difference between an official finisher and one who completes the course should be explained, to avoid the sort of disappointment I saw one newcomer express, who after practically carrying his poorly prepared bike all around the course, did not receive an award. An official finisher is normally one who completes the course having not been more than an hour overdue at any one check throughout the day. If this sounds easy, then it might be as well to pause and think.

For example, an average trail rider in a hard event might lose ten minutes on each stage. At the end of the day, if all goes well, he would not be more than 50 minutes late at the last check and so stil eligible for an award. But, supposing he stalls his bike in a river and has to fit a new sparking plug? If he took eight minutes to get his bike going again, he would be eighteen minutes late at the next check. Next, he takes on fuel, which takes up two minutes and is then held up in a narrow gulley by a fallen rider, perhaps another two minutes tick away. Totalled up, poor Fred Everyman is two minutes over the maximum allowance and although finishing the course, does not win his medal. Obviously, the rider has got to be able to keep within striking distance of his standard time if he is to have any hope of winning anything. Enduros, as may be seen, do provide a real challenge to even the most skilful and experienced rider.

During the course of the event, there may also be additional tests of riding skill such as speed hill climbs and braking and acceleration tests. These are scored on the same principle as the speed test and primarily are tie-breakers, to split the riders whose scores are very close.

If all this sounds like achieving the impossible, then try to take heart in that few, if any, riders have any immediate success in enduros, regardless of how good they are at allied sports. There are exceptions, of course. Motocross star Graham Noyce finished fourth overall in his first event — but in general, most riders find this branch of motorcycling very exacting, which is just why it is so much fun.

Most enduro courses can be ridden by the average trail rider with a reasonable machine. Initially, the newcomer should aim at just riding round the course and getting the feel of the sport. Then, as his confidence increases, he can begin chasing the medals.

It is all very well to blithely write average and reasonable, and expect these terms to have a universal value, but what do they mean in practical terms?

Before attempting an enduro, I would expect a rider who is going to enjoy himself rather than suffer an extended period of masochism, to have the confidence to handle his machine in all the situations described in Chapter 8. Not only should he be able to ride his bike, but he should have an idea of how to rescue it when it becomes stuck, for there is no guarantee that anyone will help during an event.

Enduros are physically taxing, not nearly so much as motocross, but probably more so than observed trials. Therefore it is necessary to be in sound physical condition if the event is to be fun.

Finally, I would recommend that some practice at speed riding on the rough be undertaken before entering an enduro, since it is easy for the most complete novice to be encouraged into riding faster by the scent of competition and suddenly discover that he is travelling at an unfamiliar pace. Most riders like to have a good thrash at some stage in the event and it increases the fun if you are in a position to do this.

You will, I hope, notice that I keep repeating the phrase "if it is to be fun". There is no law against entering an enduro with a brand new pseudo-motocross moped and an experience of rough riding that amounts to driving down a gravel path. Just don't expect organisers to design a suitable course for you; you can be sure they won't.

There are a number of such competitors in every event and sure enough, they are to be found with wrecked bikes, exhausted and dejected after the first few miles. If this is your idea of fun, then please ignore the previous comments. I came into enduros from motocross and so had ample experience of rough riding but if I were new to the sport, I would give myself a sporting chance of finishing before I entered an event. Otherwise, why bother? If you can handle your bike confidently on a rutted muddy lane and deal with a few rocks — even at low speeds — then have a go and enjoy yourself. If not, then gain a little more experience before attempting something which might colour your opinion unfavourably for some time to come.

The same code of conduct applies to machines. If your bike will complete a day's trail riding without any problems, then it is good enough for an enduro. You are not going to win a Gold medal in the ISDT on anything else other than an expensive and sophisticated racing machine, but it is possible to take home a Bronze medal in a British event, on a soundly prepared trail bike. However, if your machine suffers from water in the ignition, or the chain is so worn that it jumps the sprockets, or it won't rev. hard enough to get up steep hills, then you are doing no more than inviting a mass of trouble by subjecting it to the rigours of competition. Enduros will test even carefully prepared and tuned competition machines — they will decimate the ranks of clumsily prepared trail bikes.

In order to enter an enduro, a competitor has to be a member of an A-CU — affiliated club. There are certain clubs, such as the Caerleon or the Welsh Trail Riders Association, which are very involved with enduros, and for those riders who have access to organisations such as these, there will be a wealth of information and help to hand. A second best alternative is to join a club which is involved with motocross or trials since it will contain members of a sporting inclination who will be able to offer some advice, even if they have not actually competed in enduros themselves.

By looking in the sporting guide of the weekly motorcycle papers it is quite a simple matter to find a local motocross or trial and from then on it is just as easy to find a member oi the organising club, who will be only too delighted to relieve you of the membership fee, enrol you and probably trick you into helping out on the spot.

For all A-CU events, you will need a competition licence and an A-CU approved crash helmet, but other than these formalities, enduros are very relaxed and easy going. All that remains is to keep an ear to the ground regarding a forthcoming event — your fellow club members will help you in this task — enter quickly, for the number of available places is limited and they are very soon taken, and prepare for battle. In the next Chapter, we will have a look at some of the ways of not only finishing, but collecting an award as well.

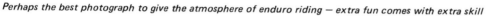

Perhaps the best photograph to give the atmosphere of enduro riding — extra fun comes with extra skill

A body belt is very useful in an enduro

11 Getting serious

Although I manage to win medals on a fairly regular basis — which proves the power of prayer, if nothing else — I find enduros hard work. Watching Mick Bowers and Dave Jeremiah fly up frozen, vertical hills without even touching a foot down, one would think that enduros were just like riding around the park. Observing a rider like myself struggle up the same climb, with legs dead from exhaustion, gives a truer picture.

Not being an ISDT star does have the advantage of knowing exactly how the not-so-expert rider reacts in a desperate situation, so that many of the comments made will be of particular interest to those fairly inexperienced riders who, having read the previous Chapter and thinking that enduros sound like fun, decide to have a go themselves.

Perhaps the biggest drawback to riding in enduros is that a lot of organisation is required. Through years of riding motocross, I have reached a stage where I can leave home a couple of hours before a meeting, time my entry to the track to coincide with the start of practice, then race without ruffling a feather. Enduros are not so easy.

The main problem is that the best events are, at the time of writing, usually held in Wales. My home is near Liverpool so I am not too far away but even so, to be ready for a 9.01am start, it is essential that one lives almost on top of the event if an overnight stay is to be avoided. I have tried the "leave at 2am and have a nap on the way" approach but personally, I find this unsatisfactory. Even worse, it can be dangerous, for enduros are a demanding sport at best, without riding in a state of near-exhaustion from lack of sleep.

Similarly, I find the thought of camping out appalling, although to many competitors, it is as much fun as the event. The thought of riding all day in the rain until the water has seeped through to one's bones and then settling down to a night's sleep in a damp tent just does not appeal, but like travelling through the night, personal preference must be the over-riding factor.

The organising club will issue a list of hotels in the area of the trial and it is advisable to book a bed early if you intend doing the job in style. For example, 150 riders are going to descend on Caerleon for the ISCA 150 trial, and perhaps 75-100 will need to stay overnight. I am not sure how many beds there are available, but to my knowledge there are only one or two small hotels in the town — one of which is rather chic and consequently expensive — and I am sure they do not have the sort of capacity needed to house all the riders. Immediately your entry is despatched, book a bed and then worry about the consequences of cancelling it if you do not get a ride. This is far better than groping around the night before the event, knocking on doors like a latter day Joseph of Nazareth.

Because the trial is held at a long distance from home base, it will usually be impractical to ride the bike to the start. This means that you will have to be carried in a van or trailer. Should you decide to become a regular enduroist, then either of these two modes of transport may be regarded as an economic proposition for not only will they provide transport to meetings but they will also encourage more serious trail riding in a region different from one's own immediate locality. I am very lucky in that both the Pennines and Wales are within bike riding distance, but a rider based in one of the major connurbations, particularly in the South East, would need some means of transporting his bike to any of the better trail riding regions of the West Country or Wales. Similarly, I keep promising myself a couple of days up in Scotland, and for this exercise, I would definitely need to carry the bike to the general area in which I wanted to ride.

Until you are committed, the best way of dealing with the problem of transportation is to find a couple of like-minded riders and collectively hire a van. Many firms do a cheap weekend rate, and if the vehicle were not taken until Friday night, and returned by Monday morning, the cost, divided three or four ways, will be very reasonable. A Ford Transit or Bedford CF will take three bikes and equipment comfortably, and four at a squeeze, which is adequate capacity for a team effort.

Travelling in this manner also solves another problem, that of pit-crew. This term has wonderful racy connotations and can range from a highly skilled Czech team member counting down the seconds until his rider enters the control, in perfect time, to a spectator who has been reluctantly press ganged into service, sloshing half a gallon of petrol over a cursing rider.

The quality of the pit crew usually parallels the skill and success of the rider — although not always — so as a newcomer, do not expect the sort of service an ISDT rider will get. I have had some excellent pit crews who have made up in their abundant enthusiasm what they lacked in experience; so much so that their attentions have often been an embarrassment after a mediocre ride.

Left Some method of transporting a bike to an enduro is essential. It also helps when planning green lane runs in the more remote and exciting parts of Great Britain. One of the best methods of doing this is by using a trailer

The ubiquitous Ford Transit

The Custom van has a bulkhead which cuts noise considerably. Inside, there is ample room for three bikes

A Bedford CF van, well loaded with three bikes and all the gear for a day's trail riding. Split three ways, the cost of hiring a van can be reasonable

All that is needed for a novice's assistant is someone who will, WITHOUT FUSS, fill the rider's bike with petrol whilst the rider oils the chain, pass a clean pair of goggles and tell him how well he is doing. And when he returns, congratulations on having made it back and commiserations regarding any misfortunes. What you do not want is a too-keen type who treats the rider like a works runner and leaps around shouting orders and generally making a fuss. I once had a friend of this sort who crewed for me — he was a road racer and presumably took his sport very seriously — and shouted and urged me on to even greater efforts with much gesticulating and rushing around the bike. He rushed around so much that he didn't fill the bike full of petrol and I ran out of fuel in the middle of the forest. To add insult to injury, I was having a good ride and might well have taken home a medal. Of course it was my own fault for being bullied and not checking that there was enough petrol in the tank but this sort of assistant can be most disconcerting for the average rider, and even, I have been told, the expert.

If you can offer a free trip to a fellow trail rider who is not competing then you will have an ideal pit crew. However, even if you do not have your own assistant, one of the more experienced teams can always be persuaded to take petrol and a spare pair of goggles for you, along with their own supplies. Enduros are a very friendly sport and I don't think I could imagine anyone being left to struggle on their own.

Having said that you will be likely to get help at an enduro, don't expect it as a birth-right. If you get stuck out on the course, someone will undoubtedly render assistance — eventually — but in all fairness, you can't expect a fellow competitor to screech to a halt in order to help you. If the event is to be enjoyable, you should give yourself every chance of finishing by ensuring that your bike is thoroughly prepared.

In addition to the work normally undertaken for a hard trail ride, take extra care over waterproofing. Make sure that the electrical system is sealed at every joint with silicone rubber sealant and that none of the wires are chafing on the frame. If your bike has points, coil and condenser, then make sure that all the connections are tight but not so much that the wire is weakened. Similarly, check that the earth wire is sound.

Normally, if a bike is running well and it stops through electrical trouble, a broken wire will be the fault. Any deterioration of the component parts in an ignition system is gradual and the trouble will manifest itself before the event in difficult starting or mis-firing. This being the case, familiarize yourself with the main wiring pattern from the generator to the coil/condenser and then on to the sparking plug. If you do strike trouble, then you will know how to check quickly for the offending break.

A typical scene at an enduro, with good crews working efficiently to help their riders. This is the ideal to aim for — a beginner will be lucky if his crew comes up to these standards

The second most common problem is petrol starvation. If an engine has fuel and a spark, then it will run. Not necessarily well, but it will function. Deprive it of either one of these two things and it will stop. If you do come to a halt on the trail, and the bike is not suffering either from electrical or fuel troubles, then there is not much you can do to remedy the situation, for a broken gearbox mainshaft, or a cracked piston, is not suitable for repair in the middle of the forest.

Make sure that the bike's air filtration system works effectively and that a fuel filter, which will stop water from entering the carburettor, is fitted. Check all air-filter joints and the junctions between the carburettor and air-filter box, since water often finds its way in through one of these weak spots.

Despite all these precautions, water can still occasionally penetrate the carburettor. If the rider is lucky, it will lie at the bottom of the float bowl and cause no trouble but a blob of moisture in a nasty frame of mind can block the main jet of the carburettor. To minimize this trouble, make sure that if a main jet filter is provided, it is fitted in good condition. Also, practise stripping and rebuilding the carburettor before the meeting, so the procedure is familiar. Finally, make sure that you have suitable tools for removing the main jet carried on the bike. Fortunately, if a blocked jet does occur, the water can easily be removed with a healthy blow and providing the rider is able to remove the jet quickly, the whole exercise need not take long.

Pit stops are always very busy but should not be hectic. Note that this Maico rider and his assistant are working calmly and efficiently on the bike. This is the key to fast repairs in the field. Close to hand are his petrol, funnel, chain lube and a bottle of water, all he is likely to need

All nuts on the bike should be checked for tightness and those which are vulnerable to vibration, such as the ones retaining the expansion chamber, should be drilled and wired. I do use chemical locking agents, such as Loctite, but for really critical applications, I still prefer to drill and wire. Properly applied, there is no question of a chemical locking agent failing, but the sight of a length of copper coated wire passing through the nut and bolt gives me visual comfort, which is most satisfying. Using Loctite, I know intellectually that the nut is safe; wiring it on, I can see and feel that it is not going to vibrate loose — which is much better psychologically.

The gearbox drain plug and sump plate on a four-stroke machine should always be wired in place for if the thousand to one chance of losing one of these nuts should turn up, not only will the engine be wrecked through lack of lubricant, but should the seizure occur at an inopportune moment, then a nasty fall could result. Certainly, the thought of the Suzuki's gearbox locking solid when I am flat out in fourth gear is not an appealing thought.

In addition to having some idea of how to rectify electrical or fuel faults, the rider should be able to fit replacement cables to his bike and these should be carried on the machine, ready for use. I go out in an enduro ready to race and try and win a medal and in doing this, I am prepared to take some chances. For example, I would ride without either a front or rear brake if a cable broke and I was having difficulty keeping on time, effecting the repair after the next check or even at the end of the event, if I was within striking distance of home.

With this in mind, I keep the spare clutch and front brake cable coiled up on the handlebars ready for use but not fitted over the cable in use, as do some riders. This is because I prefer to have the lightness of operation that a single cable, free to flex, affords and I am prepared to ride on in an emergency until such time as I can spare two minutes to fit a new cable. Both the clutch and front brake are accessible on my Suzuki so there is no real hardship in routing a new cable but on some bikes, it might well be essential to have a spare cable in place. Obviously, the cables should be in good condition and the exposed ends sealed with pvc tape. Whilst not a world beater, I am a competent rider with enough experience to ride without brake or clutch and live to tell the tale. A novice might not have sufficient skill to manage this and could harm himself, so it is up to the rider to make a value judgement of his own ability and either press on, or stop and put the bike back in perfect condition. Always err on the side of safety, for to succeed in enduros, you have to be there at the end, and not stuck half way up a tree on a special test.

One cable which is essential to have in place is the throttle. I have this ready for a quick changeover and I have practised swopping cables until the operation is automatic. Remember you may be working under very adverse conditions and it is imperative that you know exactly how to work on the bike, if your stop is to be a brief one.

It is surprising what can be bent back to shape after a fall and with a little ingenuity, handlebars, gearlevers, brake pedals and all the other vulnerable bits can be persuaded back into service. Footrests should be folding wherever possible, for not only will they be safer, but less prone to damage.

My final word regarding machine preparation is to be meticulous. Let your friends mock you for being fussy but check, re-check and then check the checks, until you are perfectly satisfied that the bike is right. In doing this, not only will you increase your chances of finishing, but just as important, by knowing that the bike is right, you will be happy in your mind and ride that much better.

In a category on their own come tyres, for punctures are one of the enduro riders' worst enemies. It is essential to carry a spare tube for both the front and rear tyre and be able to fit them, even if it is a struggle, merely so that you can ride back to civilisation.

I loathe changing tyres but when leading my class in the 1975 Wayfarers enduro I got a series of punctures. Motivated by the urgency of the situation, and aided by the quickly detachable wheels on the Fantic I was riding, I managed to change a tyre, and get back on the move, in seven or eight minutes. This is not brilliant when compared with the sub-four-minute times of the experts but does show that with sufficient desperation, even tyre fitting can be achieved in a reasonable time.

Positive wiring of vulnerable nuts is of psychological as well as practical value

There are three essentials for the job, other than the spare tube. The first is a set of **good** tyre levers which you know will remove a thick-walled knobbly tyre. Second is a tin of compressed liquid rubber latex (which will mend small holes in the tube without removing the tyre) sold under the trade name "Finilec". This comes in an aerosol container and will quickly inflate a tyre to about 18psi, more than enough pressure for enduros. The third requirement for fast tyre changing is a set of quickly detachable wheels — the Italian firm of Grimeca make an excellent pair — and if you were a really serious and successful competitor, it would be worth the expense of converting an existing machine. I am prepared to struggle with the Suzuki in the event of a puncture and I think most riders of less than top expert calibre would be of the same opinion. Jawa machines however, have qd wheels fitted as standard.

Finilec can inflate even a 5.00" x 18" tyre to 15 psi in just a few seconds. It is also possible to repair small punctures without removing the tube

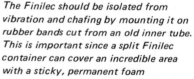

The Finilec should be isolated from vibration and chafing by mounting it on rubber bands cut from an old inner tube. This is important since a split Finilec container can cover an incredible area with a sticky, permanent foam

Matters can be helped considerably by fitting a proper ISDT tyre of the type described in Chapter 5. These tyres are not only much less prone to concussion bursts (a puncture caused by the tube splitting under impact, for example when hitting a rock ledge at high speed) but can also be ridden flat for considerable distances and at surprisingly high speeds. However, once again, I would recommend caution, for whilst a professional rider might be able to control the bike at 60mph, snaking, a lesser mortal attempting the same speed on a deflated tyre would get himself into a terrible tangle. And on this matter, I speak from personal experience.

In addition to spare tubes and cables, such spares and spanners as might be needed to carry out emergency repairs will have to be carried on the bike. Not only will there not be too many garages on the top of a Welsh sheep track but the regulations of most enduros specifically state that it is forbidden to use any tools other than those carried on the bike. In practice, this regulation might be interpreted as meaning not using any tools except those carried on the bike and getting caught in the act. What the eye does not see, the heart does not grieve over.

Every attempt should be made to carry the minimum possible because every ounce on the bike makes riding that much more difficult. It is essential to have the following:

1   Plug spanner and spare plug. More than one if your bike is giving trouble in this direction.
2   Spanners to remove both wheels.
3   Spanner to re-adjust the handlebars.
4   Spanner to tighten up exhaust system retaining nuts.
5   Spanners to fit new cables.
6   Screwdrivers to remove points and/or air-filter hose clamps.
7   Pair of pliers.
8   Pair of Mini-Mole grips.

Very often, the same spanner will do more than one job and so the total amount taken need only be small. Many European bikes use preferred sizes and so most of the machine will be held together by nuts and bolts having an across-the-flats size of 10mm or 13mm. With an open-ended and ring spanner in each of these sizes it was almost possible to fit a new crankshaft in the Fantics I raced and the bike could almost be rebuilt on the side of the road. The Suzuki I ride at present uses a massive range of nuts and bolts and poses much more of a problem. Check your bike, think about the jobs you will have to tackle and then take the minimum necessary and the planning will pay dividends.

Similarly with screwdrivers. If it is possible to carry just one medium sized screwdriver, then do so. But first, in the peace and security of the workshop, check to see that there is not some vital connection that can only be tightened by a fine screwdriver and think how you will curse if you don't have one in your tool bag when the need arises in an event.

Pliers are an essential for bending and squeezing things which are misbehaving and I also include Mini-Mole grips in my tool kit. These are small, self-locking pliers which will tenaciously grip anything to which they are applied. For example, they would function quite satisfactorily as an emergency gearlever or as a nipple on the end of a broken clutch cable. As an emergency life-belt, they are invaluable.

I also carry the following bits and pieces which I have found from experience, can be useful:

1   Roll of pvc insulation tape.
2   Small coil of annealed wire suitable for holding wayward bits on the bike.
3   Spare front brake lever, which will also fit the clutch if turned upside down.
4   A square of clean, absorbent rag.
5   Small length of electrical wire with the ends bared ready for use.
6   One or two set bolts carrying several nuts in sizes applicable to the bike.
7   Two spare split links.

If I can't mend the bike with this selection, and the tools that I carry, then I will be stuck with a number of major problems, the first of which will be rescuing the bike.

Dependent on how tolerant the rider is to personal privations, almost any clothing can be used for enduros, with the exception of the safety helmet, which must be A-CU approved for use in competition. This is a rather silly situation since a novice rider in a club scramble, who will probably never reach a speed in excess of 25 miles an hour, will have to wear leather jeans, or an approved leather substitute, A-CU approved shirt and gloves. However, that same rider can compete in an enduro — where there is far more opportunity for an inexperienced

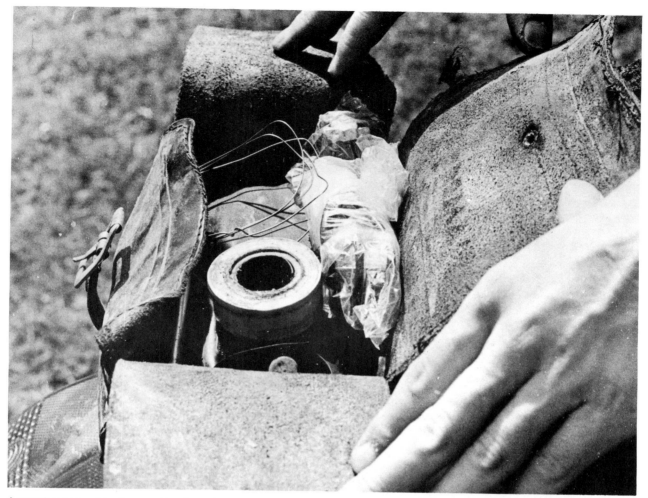

A complete array of tools as used by the author in the Welsh Two Day. Note that there is sufficient to deal with any repair less than that requiring full workshop facilities — but no more. The number of tools should be carefully thought out and kept to the absolute minimum. Note also the spare electrical cable with ends ready bared, annealed wire for emergency repairs and PVC tape

All this, and a clean absorbent rag, packs into the Suzuki's tool bag along with a chainbreaker and spare links

The place to carry a set of spare cables already oiled for use

A Grimeca qd wheel dismantled. The wheel can be removed from the swinging arm in about ten seconds, which is a great help if the tyre has to be changed

Two rules to remember for fast wheel changing: 1. Tighten the wheel spindle by hand

This Italian unit is particularly good since it contains a very robust shock absorber in the hub. Note the five holes which accept the wheel pins very quickly

2. Remove it with your foot

rider to reach quite high speeds — in jeans and a cotton T-shirt, if he is so moved. This ruling is an anachronism from the time when enduros had more in common with observed trials than motocross, a situation no longer true today.

Logically, since an enduro is just as fast as a motocross race — although somewhat safer since a rider can choose his own speed and still be competitive — and the ground makes no distinction as to whether it is being used for an enduro or motocross, and consequently, is just as hard in both cases, the clothing regulations should be the same for both events.

Given suitable weather, I will wear my Kershaw G.P. motocross leathers, a thin shirt and a TT Leathers Vystram jacket. This outfit is very comfortable and will give good protection in the event of an accident. It is also proof against the occasional shower or water splashed up from a river crossing.

Standing in the paddock of a winter enduro, with sleet lashing across the hills and clouds at tree-top height, the summer outfit will just not be suitable for me. In such conditions, I wear a waxed cotton Belstaff suit with a shirt and thin pullover beneath the jacket and a pair of thick jeans between me and the trials suit trousers. Obviously, the degree of protection offered by unpadded waxed cotton is not as great as a pair of racing leathers, nor is the comfort the same, but a waxed cotton suit will keep the wearer dry and warm in the most severe conditions imaginable.

I am very lucky in having two outfits — one of which I borrow from my motocross activities — but the novice, unless he is an exceptionally well-heeled one, will be better off choosing a waxed cotton suit initially, which will earn its keep on ordinary trail rides as well as in enduros.

Whatever you choose, then make sure it is comfortable. Even a short enduro will entail five hours' riding and this can be a painfully long time if the rider's clothing pinches or is too heavy. If you are comfortable, you will be relaxed, and a relaxed rider is both faster and safer than one who is tense.

Another part of the A-CU regulations which govern clothing to be worn in enduros permits the wearing of industrial rubber boots, of the type described in Chapter 6. This is quite ridiculous since there is a distinct chance that a rider using these boots for racing — and many do — will hurt himself. Leather boots, with a proper slipper sole, are essential and should, I feel, be made obligatory for all such events. Ride in an old pvc or jeans, jacket, if you must, but clothe your head in a good glass fibre helmet and your feet in a pair of purpose designed boots and it is highly likely that you will compete unscathed for years.

A body-belt is also worth considering, unless the rider has an exceptionally good set of back and stomach muscles. Motocross gloves with anti-blister palms will make life much easier on the hands and I have noticed that lately, motocross face masks, which give good protection from flying stones, are becoming popular. I don't like them personally, since they tend to give me claustrophobia, but if you can wear one comfortably, the added protection offered must be useful.

My final word must be on goggles. Together with boots and helmet these are the most vital pieces of riding gear and should be worn wherever possible. Unfortunately, it is not always possible to wear goggles in heavy rain, or mist, so to counsel never removing them would be rather hypocritical. I have two pairs of Carrera ski goggles and change them whenever I see my pit crew so that I usually have clean goggles every fifty miles. This is a useful system to cultivate since it encourages the wearing of goggles and also relieves the rider of the time and chore of cleaning them.

So, prepared in mind, body and machine, the racing can begin.

Even world class motocross stars feel tenseness in an enduro. Graham Noyce shows all his burning desire for a medal

12 When do I get my medal?

On arriving at the start of the enduro, the first job is to present your bike for examination, where it will be checked both to see that it is road and race-worthy and complies with the regulations for the event. This is called scrutineering and after the bike has passed — it will have to be a very poorly prepared bike in a positively dangerous condition to fail — it will have to be put in a closed area called the parc fermé. Once in this area, it cannot be touched, and this includes fuelling, so make sure that your bike is ready to race in every way before entering the controlled area. Depending on the level of the event, machines will have to be in the parc fermé anything from the night before, to only half an hour, before the start.

The rider will then be given access to his machine 15 minutes before the start and he can check it over in the case of a one day event, or carry out vital and much needed maintenance in a multi-day enduro, before starting.

A marshal at the start line will call your number and the numbers of the men who will be starting with you, directly after the riders who immediately precede have left. Then there is a wait of about fifty seconds before the signal to start is given.

That fifty seconds is an infinite wait. The checks you have carried out on your bike are questioned, an imaginary roughness in the throttle cable appears as you play with the twist grip and a sideways glance at the rider next to you reveals that he is calm and confident. He has just looked at you and thought the same thing.

This tenseness should not be fear — if it is then you really should not be racing. Rather it is an anxiety to do well, coupled with a determination to finish. Merely writing this description has made the palms of my hands sweat and the adrenalin pump, for even though I have no enduros scheduled for some months, there still remains the automatic reaction to the thought of competition.

If the feeling of tenseness and excitement is absent, then you are not going to do very well, because immediately a problem occurs, it is unlikely that you will have the desire to overcome it. Many riders it seems, look for reasons to retire, and of course, very quickly find them. As the seconds tick away to the start, keep on insisting to yourself that you WILL finish and you WILL take home a medal and that absolutely nothing is going to stop you. In this frame of mind, reinforced by confidence in your machine, you will have as good a ride as your ability permits and one can ask for no more.

As the start marshal consults his watch for your starting time to appear, check that the bike is ready to go. Petrol on, choke closed and carburettor flooded. Leg poised on the kickstart, watch for the flag to drop and then two or three prods should have the motor bursting into life. Now the value of all the preparation can be seen, as the chap who was supposed to start with you is left still struggling to get his bike to fire.

Immediately you have crossed the twenty metre line, you can relax — you are now an official starter. It's a good feeling. Another 100 miles like this and that medal will be yours.

Enduros, probably more so than any other form of racing, require the rider to consciously think his way through the event, from beginning to end. Start by treating yourself, and your bike, gently in the first couple of miles and you will be amply repaid by better performance later on. Driving a cold engine flat out from absolute cold does no good at all and riding on the limit from the drop of the flag also induces rider fatigue. Take a little time to adjust yourself and the bike to the conditions but obviously not so much that you immediately penalise yourself. Riding at 75% of your racing speed is taking things easy, any less is dawdling.

It is important to remember that you may be paired with a rider who is much better than you and should

Now is the time when all the hours spent in the workshop begin to pay dividends. 163, Alan Morris, has to coax his reluctant Husqvarna into life whilst 165, A. O'Neil, and the author wait for the signal to begin their ride

you try to ride at his pace, then trouble may occur. For example, in the 1975 Welsh Two Day Trial, British Trophy Team member Ernie Page started just behind me. Not unaturally, Ernie passed me with monotonous regularity on each section (he eventually won his class and finished second overall) and had plenty of time in hand where I had little or none. If I had tried to keep pace with Page, I would have fallen — of that there is no doubt. Instead, I had to ride at my own pace, which I had decided was as fast as I could ride commensurate with avoiding exhaustion or risking a fall, which would not only be time-consuming, but also painful.

In enduros, there is no merit in beating a fellow rider out on the track and failing some time later against the clock. Having said that, should you be lucky enough to get with a rider just a little better than you, then this will be an advantage, since by following him, it will be possible to increase your speed and still ride comfortably within your limits. If this does happen, then try to stick with him whatever happens, since he will take much of the hard work out of the event by finding the best path, or line for you.

You will have already recorded your expected time of arrival on your time card and it is useful also to have these times written on a piece of masking tape stuck to the petrol tank, so that a check can be made on progress without having to fish the card out of a greasy pocket.

Checks are indicated by a white flag and then a yellow one 20 metres after it. Those who are having a good ride, will have time to spare and they will wait at the white flag until the correct time appears. Then riding forward, they will present their time card to a marshal, have it stamped and their passage recorded on a master sheet as a check, and ride on their way. However, the novice will be well advised to ride straight into the control and have his card stamped since he is unlikely to be early unless the section has been very easy.

Being paired with a rider of about your own ability can be a great help. After the early loss of a minute, Malcolm Tottle and the author had a most enjoyable ride during the first day of the 1976 Welsh Two Day Trial. Both were riding hard and fast but because of their competence and very similar riding ability both were perfectly safe. Unfortunately, Malcolm found a malevolent bog on the second day and the duel could not be renewed

Once the first check is passed, I always feel much better. Most of the hard luck stories seem to happen between the start and the first check and having passed this point is a definite achievement. If everything else goes wrong, then there is one scalp under your belt. Just another four to go to the end.

By now, it will be as well to have settled into a relaxed riding rhythm. The worse possible technique to use is one where the rider is forcing himself along in an erratic style. Instead, the ride should be pleasant, taken at a pace — no matter how fast or slow — which is smooth and conservative. Such a style is not only valid for novices but is the hallmark of a high quality rider at any level. Just watch a few of the fast men in a National Enduro and it will be immediately apparent how easy they make the task look, regardless of the fact that they are travelling very quickly.

Sooner or later, it is likely that you will strike some sort of trouble whether mechanical or one presented by the course. That this should happen is almost inevitable for the novice, since if the course did not cause trouble to the beginner, then it would be unlikely to present a challenge to the more experienced rider. This is the time when you may well discover something about your own personality, as well as your riding and mechanical abilities, for out on a deserted part of the track, you will be very much alone.

The first step is to find out exactly what is wrong. If the bike is stuck in a bog, keep calm and plan your way out of it. Perhaps it can be dragged to high land on your own, or would it be better to strike a bargain with another stranded rider? Possibly the bike has stopped. Again, think your way through the problem, for blind panic is not only futile and unproductive but it also costs time and you still want that medal, don't you? Now is the time to give up, if your resolve is weak. Now is the time that you find out whether you really want to ride in a competitive event.

I like to think that I will have a good try at sorting out whatever the problem is, since I do not like to retire in any motorcycling event and particularly in enduros, where there is only one chance in the day to finish. Having said this, let me go on to add that when you have tried your best to beat the problem and can muster no more strength, either physical or mental, then have the sense to call a halt to the proceedings and look forward to the next event. Enduros are one of the safest forms of motorcycle sport and it is only when a rider pushes himself too far that accidents are likely to occur. If the bike is stuck or stranded, it will be rescued eventually, and can always be repaired, but a rider who is damaged may not be so lucky, and there is certainly more trouble obtaining spare parts for bodies than for bikes.

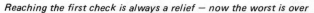

Reaching the first check is always a relief — now the worst is over

There is always a helping hand available even for the most experienced rider. Sammy Miller, probably the most successful rider in the history of motorcycling, has his card stamped and returned before speeding on his way

After a couple of hours, the event will have begun to take shape, the checks will come and go and you will begin to feel like an expert. No longer are you a novice but a fully fledged clubman rider with real racing experience.

The last 25 miles will be hard on your body, unused to such physical exertion complaining vigorously, but the end is now in sight. Through the last check and still in time, there is nothing can stop you now. Then, the finish. Relief and pleasure at having finished within the time limit — at least a Bronze medal. Now for the re-telling of the near escapes from bogs and demons and the mammoth slide you got into on the speed test and how you beat that chap with the orange suit who has been riding for years. There is no doubt in your mind, it was well worth the effort.

Although most novices would be fortunate if they had such a fairy tale ride as our mythical newcomer, the story is not beyond the bounds of possibilities. A more likely result is a retirement or running out of time, for by the very nature of things, an enduro must, if it is to be a challenge, eliminate most of the entry.

If you have been well-prepared and ridden a race within your limits then the result, whilst lacking the ecstasy of winning a medal, should nevertheless have been good fun and well worth the entry fee. If not, and you are dissuaded from entering again, then perhaps this too, is a worthwhile lesson.

Enduros represent the quintessence of trail riding — having fun riding a bike on the rough. If they are not fun, then like trail riding, avoid them.

Some of the best rides of my motorcycling life have been on trails and particularly in enduros and I love every outing. I hope you grow to, as well.

Settling into a relaxed riding rhythm is very important — regardless of the speed. Note that in both these photographs, although the author is trying hard and travelling quickly, he is clearly relaxed and riding within his abilities. This is the way to win medals — there are no awards for the fastest crash of the day

Now is the time that you will discover just how much you really want that medal

But there is usually some sort of help to hand, either in the form of another rider or a spectator

Nice and steady for the last few miles

Trail riding IS fun